Paperless Joy
PAPERLESS BUSINESS & LIFESTYLE DESIGN WITH INFORMATION AND COMMUNICATION TECHNOLOGY

"Free yourself from location & time constraints; boost productivity and enjoy a more balanced and natural lifestyle"

George Dimopoulos, PhD, MBA
ISBN: 978-0-615-24309-2

Paperless Joy: Paperless Business & Lifestyle Design with Information & Communication Technology "Free yourself from location & time constraints; boost productivity and enjoy a more balanced and natural lifestyle"

ISBN: 978-0-615-24309-2

George Dimopoulos, PhD, MBA

Cover Design: George Dimopoulos
Published by Digital Life Artist Inc.
Baltimore, MD
www.digitallifeartist.com

TABLE OF CONTENTS

ACKNOWLEDGEMENTS

I thank Christine Grillo and Stephanie Smith for editorial assistance and great ideas, Maria-Lucia Escorcio for support and paperless guidance, the many colleagues and friends I have exchanged ideas with over paperless matters. I am also grateful to those who have shared their information and experiences relating to paperless practices and information and communication technology on the Internet and other media.

FOREWORD – A PAPERLESS PERSONAL NOTE

I understand that it's not easy to "go paperless", and it does not happen overnight. Nor will it happen simply by reading about my experiences and following my recommendations. It will require practical effort and commitment. My transition to becoming paperless required a great deal of motivation that was mostly based on the realization that it would provide many advantages in different aspects of my life—and I'll outline those in this book.

Because information and communication technology (ICT) -based paperless practices are totally dependent on available technology, it's only in the last five to ten years that it has become feasible to "go paperless." Back in the 1980s, I had my first real experience with the contrast between paper-based and paperless practices; this was during my college years in Sweden. I wrote my first research report on the medicinal use of the herb *Dictamnus* on a typewriter. I must have typed the same paragraphs and entire sections several times before I got them right, and I would spend hours, or even days, cutting sections with scissors and gluing them together into chapters, and finally the report itself had to be photocopied to make the cut and paste seams disappear. This was a very tedious process and consumed a lot of valuable time that I might have used for research, thinking, or anything else more creative and pleasant.

A couple of years later, I had to write my second comprehensive report on research that I had done in Stockholm on how muscle fibers contract. This time I used my first personal computer, and the difference was like night and day. I could change the text over and over again without having to write it from scratch each time, and I could also bring the document with me on a floppy drive and work on it using the university computers. Later, during my graduate studies in Crete, I started to use email and could instantly and without any cost communicate with friends and collaborators. For my doctoral thesis on the molecular biology of malaria-transmitting mosquitoes, I was able to use graphics software to create some of the figures, instead of employing an artist who would draw them by hand.

Several years later, during my postdoctoral training in Germany, I had my second most important realization about how much a paperless workstyle could offer — I started to use my first PDA to manage my time, contacts and notes. I no longer needed to worry about losing my calendar, because the data had been backed up on a computer. I had almost unlimited space for contact addresses and associated notes, and I did not need to write all around the corners of the page whenever a contact changed. One of the best things was that the calendar would use an alarm to remind me of upcoming appointments, so I did not have to check it every 30 minutes. Nor did I need to try to remember whether something important was going to happen later in the day. At the end of the year, I did not need to manually transfer all my contact addresses and telephone numbers to the new calendar, and I always had all my appointments and notes from previous years available, in case I needed to go back. I could even use it to read texts that I had loaded previously or play a simple game when bored during a commute. This was probably one of my most profound realizations that ICT provided me with paperless flexibility that made my life easier in many ways.

During this period, I also got my first ultra-light laptop, which enabled me to become mobile and perform work tasks on the road. When, some years later, I established my first research group in London, I started to use text messaging through cellular phones to communicate with my students and postdoctoral fellow; this was very convenient, considering that the different research facilities we were using were spread out over three different buildings on the campus. This became a very efficient way of keeping track of where everyone was and were doing. I have since then witnessed the remarkable development and advances in technology that now can provide the same computing power to a low-cost PDA as what the moon-lander required for its mission.

Over time, I have become increasingly savvy with ICT and started to use it in an increasing number of life and work activities. My current work as a professor, at Johns Hopkins University, where I study the molecular biology of tropical diseases, involves intense reading and writing tasks and also frequently takes me away on trips far from my office in Baltimore. This workstyle posed particular challenges regarding how to stay up to date with my readings, writings and communications with students, researchers and colleagues. My profession also involves gathering and processing a great deal of information, which came to me mostly in a written, paper-based format. The paper piles in my office would grow at high rates and I would every once in a while have to clean up and sort documents into either trash or file cabinets. These piles would become stressful and distracting reminders of all pending tasks, and more than once I ended up trashing things that I later regretted having thrown away.

At some point, I decided to start my transition into a paperless way of doing all my businesses. My first step toward paperlessness was to stop reading research reports in printed format on paper, but instead reading them directly from the screen. Incrementally I would get better and better at it, to the point now of now finding it easier and more natural to read from a screen than from paper.

During this transition, while inspired by a TV documentary about stockbrokers who use multiple displays to monitor the various markets, I realized that it would be much easier to read and write if I had multiple monitors. I set up a system that had three monitors connected to my computer and I can now have three or more documents or applications open at the same time. I no longer have to toggle between windows, and it would be impossible to mimic this with a paper-based system. I would obviously also do all the writing, editing and commenting on texts electronically, directly on the electronic document.

Once I became accustomed to performing all paper-based work tasks with ICT, I realized that it did not make much sense to use paper and digital documents in parallel. It would also be easier to work from home or when I was traveling if I had everything in electronic format. I bought a document scanner with an autoloader and scanned in all my paper-based documents into electronic files which I neatly organized into relevant folders on my computer. I also made one copy of all files for my laptop and one for home—and I could at this point work from any location without any compromise. When time came to buy a new laptop, I got a tablet laptop that could be used as a substitute for a paper note pad for hand writing. I gradually became 100 percent paperless, and now I only use paper when I am required to by regulations or the law. There was no use for file cabinets in my office so I got rid of those, and I decorated the empty gray walls with colored paper panels to make the environment more stimulating for creativity. Another fantastic paperless gadget is the eBook reader, which I can take with me everywhere, loaded with hundreds of books and documents.

It took me about two years to get rid of the unnecessary paper in my life and replace it with flexible ICT media, and it required a change of mindset and a lot of jumping over hurdles.... But eventually my paperlessness reduced my stress, gave me a feeling of liberation and provided a more organic lifestyle. This is good news. The *great* news is that anyone can do it. I wrote this book so that I could spread this paperless joy. I also believe that it will be much easier for you to do it, with the help of my experiences and research, which I share in this book. In fact, this book has been written in a completely paperless manner. I have used a variety of ICT and worked on it from all over the world: North, Central, and South America, Europe, Africa and Asia. I have used desktop computers, laptops, tablets and PDA-phones and a variety of means to communicate the files between my different devices and locations and my editor. I have written this book from my home and work office, trains, busses, airplanes, cars, dentists' waiting rooms, cafés, and even while walking by taking audio notes. I have used typing, digital handwriting and speech recognition software to write this book and communicated it with people through email, memory sticks and portable hard drives. And finally, I have never printed this book to work on it or read it from a paper.

While technology is often associated with something cold and lifeless, the last thing I would wish to promote is a replacement of human interactions with technology. Hence the technologies and applications addressed in this book should not be used to estrange us from each other, but enable us to get closer to each other through more effective communication and by freeing up time and providing flexibilities that will allow us to spend more time with our close friends and family. These technologies are not being developed to replace human interactions, but to enhance them.

In this book, I am not suggesting that everyone should quit his/her or her job and get on the road with a laptop and a smartphone to embark on a new life as a nomad freelance entrepreneur. I do, however, know that those who introduce paperless practices in their daily work routines will be able to enjoy many of the advantages that are outlined in this book. I do not promote paperless practices over paper-based because I think paper is a bad medium for writing and reading, but simply because ICT offers alternatives that are more versatile and thereby provide superior functionalities. While I recommend a nearly 100 percent paperless workstyle, because I think this will in the long run be the most efficient and effective, it is not necessary to abandon paper completely, but instead establish a balance between ICT-based media and paper-based media.

I am addressing paperlessness from many aspects and angles in this book—the individual, organizational, corporate, societal and global—because all these levels are interrelated and changes in one will eventually affect the other, and so forth. It will be easier to find motivation and justify the effort when it becomes clear how this change in behavior will match overall organizational and global changes that are about to come. The early adopters of paperless practices will enjoy a leading position, instead of following and reacting to environmental pressures; leading is always better than following or reacting.

George Dimopoulos, August 2008

INTRODUCTION

In the last 75 years, dramatic leaps in technology have altered the ways we gather information, what we do with it and how we communicate. During the same time period, travel has evolved at an unprecedented pace. These advances have happened so quickly, in fact, that they have outpaced our ability to adapt to—and benefit from—their potential to improve our work and personal lives. But if we could somehow "catch up," and take full advantage of these groundbreaking technologies and concepts, we could transform our business practices and our lives. These advances promise to make our lives more natural, more environmentally friendly and more productive—but first we have to learn how to use the technology wisely.

What is information technology, exactly? The Information Technology Association of America (ITAA) has defined information technology (IT) in the electronic era as "the study, design, development, implementation, support or management of computer-based information systems, particularly software applications and computer hardware." If a process involves the use of computers and software to create, convert, store, manage, transmit and retrieve information securely in a paperless manner, then it is considered an IT process. Recently, the term has been broadened to include electronic forms of communication, giving us the term information and communication technology, or ICT.

The impact of paperless ICT is profound—technological advances have the power to transform our personal lives, to change business and organizational operations, and to affect (and improve) the global economy. The rapid dissemination of ICT is revolutionizing economic and social development worldwide, especially in the developing world, where ICT has so much to contribute toward education, governance, public health, business, and decreasing the gap between the poor and rich.

But more importantly, everyone can benefit from paperless ICT. When deliberated from the tangible constraints of the traditional office, most of us can use paperless ICT to transform a 9-to-5 work- and lifestyle into something more flexible, and most of us can do so while remaining just as, or more, productive. Better yet, with the proper use of ICT, we can work while "stationed" at our favorite locations, perhaps with family and friends, without the need to commute.

These changes in individual work- and lifestyles eventually will affect not only organizations and businesses, but society as a whole. There will be profound changes at a personal, or micro, level, and at an organizational, corporate and societal, or macro, level. Each individual change toward an ICT-enabled paperless work/life "freestyle" will contribute toward transformations at the macro level, and changes at the organizational level will conversely also influence at the individual level; hence the change is driven from both directions. But every motivation for change begins in the mind, and an understanding of these broader impacts will be essential for getting you started, and for driving you through the process.

In the near future, these changes in working and living styles will not be optional, but necessary. Unprecedented change—a revolution, perhaps— is under way, and ICT is here to stay.

Driving these changes in work- and lifestyle are five major trends:

1. The easy availability of ICT such as computers, Internet and telecommunication devices.
2. The gradual shift towards a knowledge-based economy that is centered around the generation, trade and exchange of knowledge and information services and products.
3. The ever-growing urban centers with clogged highways, and the increased costs of housing and office space.
4. Long and burdensome commutes, increasing energy and fuel prices, and the environmental detriment caused by commuting cars and office facilities maintenance.
5. A universal need for improved quality of life for millions of people worldwide.

In order to maintain compatibility and competitiveness with the rest of the world, at the individual and organizational level, we have to embrace the change. Some of you may have achieved some degree of paperlessness already. But for most of us, there are still plenty of novel concepts and applications that can be implemented, and there are more opportunities for creating the freedom to earn a living through a more organic and less stressful lifestyle, through paperless joy.

WHAT THIS BOOK OFFERS AND HOW TO READ IT

My principal aim in writing this book is to provide guidance on how to use ICT to achieve what I call "paperless joy." When I use this term, I have these goals in mind:

- To work less while being more productive.
- To enjoy life more through a liberation from the tyrannies of the constraints imposed by location and time.
- To reduce the clutter in your life and get things done.
- To become more environment friendly.
- To prepare for the future.

I believe that this guide can benefit everyone, regardless of the type of work s/he or she performs. While this guidance may be most useful to those who earn their living through office-based practices, people who earn their living by performing work that is confined to a specific location and to specific schedules can also gain opportunities to improve the quality of their lives by reading this book.

I intend to convince and motivate readers to realize the unprecedented opportunities that are provided by flexible, ICT-enabled paperless practices, or paperless joy. I'll address interesting features and advantages of this work- and lifestyle transformation at the individual, organizational and societal levels, and I'll provide detailed practical guides on how to achieve them. I'd also like to offer a historical perspective of ICT evolution and to explain how advances in knowledge and information documentation and dissemination methods have led, time and again, to broader societal progress throughout history. This book will inform readers about the technologies and concepts that have changed the way we work, communicate and organize our lives in profound ways over the last 30 years.

I've organized this book in a way that does not necessarily require you to read every chapter, or to read them in order. Some of you may already be familiar with some of its topics and may therefore find it useful to read only selected sections that seem relevant to your goals. But I think you'll gain the most insight by reading the entire book. The book is a guide on how to use ICT to live and work paperlessly, without location and time constraints, but throughout it I've tried to elaborate on the many advantages of revolutionizing your work- and lifestyle, and one of the reasons I do this is to provide the steady inspiration, motivation and reinforcement that can help you to shed your old habits and adopt a new way of working and living.

A key step toward gaining leverage from ICT is figuring out how to make all of our advanced hardware and software—our gadgets—work together. By making our technologies compatible, we truly actualize their potential to transform our lives. It's true of gadgets as of many other things in life: the sum is greater than the parts. But consider how ineffectually the manufacturers of ICT enable compatibility. For example, whenever we purchase or use a new ICT device or application, each is accompanied by a comprehensive user manual, but the manufacturer provides only limited guidance on how to integrate products for improved life and work quality. When we, for instance, purchase a laptop, we know that its portability can allow us to use it from multiple locations, but we are left alone to figure out the other necessary ICT that we need to use, as well as the changes in work practices that we need to make in order to implement a true shift toward a flexible location and time working style.

Another essential step in taking full advantage of ICT—and implementing a work/life "freestyle" or "paperless joy"—is to decrease the use of and dependence on paper. In chapters to follow, I'll explain at greater length how to liberate yourself from paper-based documents and practices, how to "go paperless."

In this book, I'll provide such guidance, at a practical level. I'll give you the practical means for gaining a competitive edge and improving your life through ICT, but I'll also offer a theoretical background for adopting an ICT-enabled work/life freestyle.

Some terms may be new for some readers, and their explanations can be found in the glossary at the end. Since ICT evolves at a very fast pace and it would be impossible to maintain this book up to date with guidance on specific devices, brands, models and system, I provide some information on specific systems and application on my blog at http://enjoypaperless.blogspot.com/.

PART ONE
THEORY AND INCENTIVES

1. ICT IS CHANGING OUR WORLD TOWARDS PAPERLESS

Have you ever thought about how much your life has become, and is, influenced by information and communication technology, or how it would be without them? Imagine the world without computers, Internet and cell phones.

Throughout history, the generation of, access to, and dissemination of knowledge and information have acted as the main drivers for progress and development. In fact, with every breakthrough designed to facilitate dissemination of and access to knowledge and information, historical leaps were made in society, science and the arts. In contrast, the repression of both the flow of information and the expression of ideas has resulted in diminished competitiveness and development. This pattern is evident both at the societal and personal levels.

While knowledge is initially synthesized through human investigation, thought and imagination, its longevity is affected by successful documentation, organization and communication of ideas. In order for thoughts to persist and be used as building blocks for further ideas, and finally knowledge, they must be documented efficiently. Therefore, progress depends on the medium and means by which we express and document our knowledge and our creative endeavors. The more efficiently we can document, organize, archive and communicate our ideas, the more efficiently we can unleash our creativity, generate theories and spread them. Because they capture, preserve, evolve and disseminate history, thoughts and observations, documents and documentation technology are essential tools. They are the means by which information is made available to those who need it, when and where they need it.

The impact of efficient generation and flow of information has become particularly prominent in recent times through the emergence and domination of the knowledge economy. The main characteristic of this new economy is that production and services are based on knowledge-intensive activities. It has been argued that in the past 30 years, the leading edge of the economy in developed countries has become driven by technologies based on the production and dissemination of knowledge and information. These new technologies have experienced a particularly marked expansion since the 1950s through the proliferation of computers, and with the more recent and widespread use of electronic communications such as the Internet and wireless telephony, they have expanded further. Concurrent with these trends, a significant transition has occurred in advanced industrial nations, as they shift from manufacturing-based economies to services-driven economies. But even the classical manufacturing-based industries have adopted and greatly benefited from ICT, in ways that have led to increased labor productivity and better working conditions.

The transition into the knowledge economy is accelerating rapidly, and has been for the last thirty years. Enabling this remarkable expansion of information economics are several developments: (1) the increase in (computer) processing power, (2) the increase in communication speed and (3) the number of connected users on the Internet. These three factors have moved us very quickly from the industrial age to the information age. The knowledge-based economy renders knowledge and information as commodities—and the trade of these commodities is unaffected by geography. Distance no longer determines cost, and location does not impose constraints on production or labor. This leads to a profound change in the patterns of international trade, the notions of national borders, and assumptions about where people can live and work. In essence, the knowledge economy enables workers to produce, trade and deliver products in a location and time independent manner. We no longer need to adapt our daily, weekly and yearly life-rhythms to typical work schedules, such as 9 to 5, nor do we need to perform the work at specific locations, such as office cubicles. One essential prerequisite of this new location and time flexible work- and lifestyle is to use paperless work practices. The frequent physical relocation of our work office and the efficient communication of documents would be impossible to achieve in a paper-based manner.

Going paperless means replacing traditional paper-based practices (such as writing, note-taking, reading, editing, communicating, and even drawing) with electronic methods that take advantage of ICT devices and software—in ways that benefit us, our organizations and the environment. As ICT continues to develop rapidly, so too do the number of paperless practices. Paperless workstyles and ICT are linked intimately and interdependently, where the one assumes the other; paperless work- and lifestyles cannot be implemented without ICT, and the use of ICT naturally leads to paperlessness.

In fact, the use of ICT in conjunction with paper-based work practices becomes redundant and even inefficient in the context of a pure ICT-based paperlessness. So why do we continue to use paper, and so much of it? The explanation lies in years of conditioning, as well as a lack of appreciation for what one can achieve with ICT.

Yet, the advent of personal computers and printers has made it so easy to print electronic documents that we are seeing a dramatic increase in the consumption of paper—and often paperless workstyles are questioned or criticized for not being able to reproduce the advantages specific to paper.

Despite all criticism of and skepticism about replacing paper with digitization, though, we have all embarked already on the journey to paperless work- and lifestyles, to a greater or lesser degree. Anyone who has used email, or read a news article through the Internet, or used a digital camera to take pictures that are stored in an electronic photo album, or posted an ad on the Internet, has started not only to *use* paperless practices, but also to appreciate their superiority over the traditional paper-based practices.

While it is certainly true that paper has certain qualities that are superior to electronic media, we have to consider the tradeoffs when choosing one over the other. The advantages of replacing paper-based practices with digital ones are numerous, and will be increasing as the electronic substitutes of paper become more advanced and more refined. Here are a few of the most important benefits:

- Enjoy flexible work schedules and generate more free time.
- Enjoy a greater freedom of mobility and a lesser need to travel.
- Gain greater control of your private and personal businesses.
- Enjoy cost savings.
- Enable safer document archiving.
- Become more productive and efficient through a clutter-free and flexible workstyle.
- Adopt environmentally responsible practices.

Our world and the way we live and earn our living has already experienced dramatic changes, thanks to ICT and other technologies, in the past 30 years. The ever accelerating pace of technological development can only dictate a continuation of this change process which will lead us to a quite different way of doing business and enjoying life. Paperless joy will then be an integral part of our daily activities. You will benefit from the many advantages and be better prepared for the future by joining the paperless joy movement now.

2. THE EVOLUTION OF ICT: PAPYRUS TO ELECTRONIC MEDIA

A consequence of rapid technological development is often a difficulty in assimilating to the various applications that evolve from these, and understanding their basic functionalities. While all of us have ended up using ICT devices and systems to the point where we have become totally dependent on these, most of us have not a simple clue on how we ended up with this dependency and how these ICT function. Knowing the history behind the invention and development of methods and technologies that have changed the way we live and work will help us to better appreciate them. Understanding some of the basic concepts and features of ICT can help us making a better use of the associated applications.

A. How we got here

Information technology (IT) in the electronic era has been defined as "the study, design, development, implementation, support or management of computer-based information systems, particularly software applications and computer hardware" by the Information Technology Association of America (ITAA). Information technology can also be defined as any approach and technology used to achieve input, processing, output and communication of information—and this definition is not restricted to electronics -based devices. In a sense, IT is an ancient concept that has been redefined and refocused in the electronic era.

Information technology has evolved over several distinct periods that include the pre-mechanical, mechanical, electromechanical, and the current electronic era. Importantly, ICT development has been intertwined with the progress of both individuals and society, and without ICT you would not be able to read these words.

<u>The pre-mechanical period</u> spanned broadly from 3000 BCE to 1450 CE and it ushered in the first communications through speech and drawings. At 3000 BCE, the cuneiform was developed by the Sumerians in Mesopotamia using a stylus that could scratch marks in wet clay, and at about 2000 BCE, the Phoenicians created a symbols alphabet to which the Greeks later added vowels. The Romans gave the letters Latin names to

create the Latin alphabet. The pre-mechanical era also included the ancient Egyptian, Chinese and Greek writing media and techniques. The first 1-9 numbering systems were developed by the Egyptians while the numbering systems similar to those we use today were invented by Hindus in India between 100 and 200 CE.

The word *paper,* from the Greek (*papyros),* was originally used to describe the writing medium papyrus. The Egyptians made papyrus from flattened strips of papyrus plants as early as 3000 BCE and, because the papyrus used by western cultures was a more effective writing medium than the less flexible bamboo used in China up until the Han Dynasty, some historians believe that ancient Chinese culture was less developed than the West prior to the Han Dynasty. In 283 BCE, the Egyptians founded the Library of Alexandria, which is believed to have held, at one point, over a half million documents from Assyria, Egypt, Greece, India, Persia and many other nations. More than 100 scholars lived and performed research in the library. The destruction of this library, the ancient world's greatest archive, is considered one of the largest losses of knowledge in recorded history. If saved, some believe, our world might have looked different today.

Because the papyrus plant requires subtropical growth conditions, it was replaced outside of Egypt by parchment, a material made of processed sheepskin or calfskin. Paper, in a more similar form to what we use today, was invented by the Chinese circa 105 CE, and the earliest known printed book was made there in 868 CE. The creation of paper was not simple, and instruction in the manufacturing process was required. For quite a while, the Chinese maintained the monopoly on paper production by guarding the secret to its manufacture and by eliminating other centers of production. This enabled China to advance in culture and sciences beyond other nations. The defeat of the Chinese in the Battle of Talas in 751 CE, as well as increased trade, allowed the spread of the trade secret to the Middle East, where Arabs in Baghdad invented a process that made the paper sheets thicker. Iran employed a process that made thinner paper sheets, which was later adopted in India. The Arabs kept the manufacturing process a secret from the Europeans, who consequently waited several centuries to make paper. A book-making process had been independently developed in India, where the first books were written on palm leaves, hence the term "leaf" for a page of a book. This book-making process was adopted by the Koreans in 604 CE, and then by Buddhist priests in Japan circa 610 CE. The paper-making process was introduced in Northern Africa in 1100 CE, and by 1150 CE it had been brought to Spain via the Crusades. Valencia, in Spain, had the first paper mill in Europe in 1120 CE. Additional paper mills were later developed in Fabriano, Italy, in the 13th century. These mills used hemp and linen rags as a source of fiber for paper manufacturing.

The mechanical period lasted from 1450 to 1840 CE and included major advances in ICT development. Paper is recorded as being manufactured first in both Italy and Germany by 1400 CE, and in 1453 Johannes Gutenberg invented the movable metal-type printing process," in 1453, igniting the first information explosion. The advancement of the European cultures during the Renaissance was largely attributed to the invention of paper, in combination with the printing press, which allowed for large-scale production and copying of single texts. In Europe, the urban working class and even many peasants could afford popular prints on paper as early as the 1400s, while books remained relatively expensive and thereby largely inaccessible for these classes until the 19th century. The slide rule, the pascaline (mechanical calculator), Leibniz's Stepped Reckoner (digital mechanical calculator) and Babbage's engines (precursors to computers) were invented in this period and represented the first mechanical computational devices. Joseph Marie Jacquard's loom, designed during the 1830s and remarkably similar to contemporary computers, represented the first step towards the development of punch card machines.

The electromechanical period spanned from 1840 to 1940 and here the harnessing of electricity was the major advance—electricity allowed knowledge and information to be converted into electrical impulses. The voltaic battery, the telegraph, Morse code, the telephone and the radio were a series of implementations of electricity that greatly enhanced the ICT capabilities of those times. In 1880, electromechanical computing was introduced by Herman Hollerith and IBM. The first more advanced computer was the Automatic Sequence Controlled Calculator (ASCC), also known as the Mark 1, completed in 1944—it was a device eight feet tall, 51 feet long, two feet thick and five tons heavy, and it consisted of 750,000 parts that stored data and program instructions on paper rolls.

In conjunction with the invention of the fountain pen, the pencil and the steam-driven rotary printing press, wood-based paper transformed 19th century economy and society in industrialized nations. Books and newspapers became gradually accessible to all members of society by 1900, and this availability and accessibility greatly accelerated the spread of knowledge and information. Widespread availability of paper also enabled the creation of personal documents such as diaries and letters that could be exchanged and used for the transmission of knowledge and information. These advances in paper-based ICT during this and the previous mechanical period are good examples of how cost- and labor-efficient document creation and dissemination have always been essential to the development and progress of individuals, organizations and civilizations. In Chapter 14 we will see how ICT today is driving major transformations, not only in the developed world, but also in the poorer developing regions of our planet.

The electronic era began in the 1940s and is ongoing. The invention of electronic vacuum tubes in the 1940s allowed the development of the first high-speed, general-purpose electronic computer, called the Electronic Numerical Integrator and Computer (ENIAC). The first general-purpose computer for commercial use: the Universal Automatic Computer (UNIVAC) was developed in the 1950s. Four generations of digital computing broadly evolved from the 1950s through today and represent impressive technological and software advancements including vacuum tubes, transistors, integrated circuits and, finally, microprocessors, used in today's computers. Storage media has evolved from punch cards, magnetic drums, cores, tapes, discs to non-volatile memories. In tandem, computer programs and software have evolved from machine and assembly language to high-level programming languages such as FORTRAN, COBOL and others.

Over the last two decades, advances in computers and networking have revolutionized the process of creating and disseminating documents. The introduction of ICT in offices has rendered many types of secretaries redundant, and paper obsolete. Electronic documentation replaces paper by providing an unprecedented degree of flexibility, cost efficiency and security in the way we acquire, generate, archive and communicate information. In fact, this recent progress has occurred so quickly that few individuals have managed to assimilate and exploit the advances fully enough to become location and time flexible workers and live with a paperless joy.

B. Essential ICT

Several ICTs and applications have been particularly important in transforming recent history, as follows.

A microprocessor, also called a central processing unit (CPU), contains memory, logic and control circuits on a single chip. Its creation represented a milestone in modern ICT development. The microprocessor enabled the development of home-use personal computers such as PCs and Macintoshes. The first IBM PC was introduced in 1981, followed by Apple's Macintosh in 1984. Both hardware and software have experienced remarkable development since then, significantly changing the ways we go about many of our work tasks and personal businesses. However, we would never have been able to exploit the full potential of computers if not for the interconnectivity provided by the Internet.

The Internet has today evolved into the most widespread and complex high-capacity information exchange system. It all started in the 1960s, when computer researchers became interested in establishing a global network that would connect smaller local networks. Initially, this led to the development of several disjointed, separate networks, which later were connected through inter-networking protocols; multiple networks were joined together into larger networks. The spread of this ever growing inter-network into a global inter-network, later called "The Internet," was facilitated by the existing telecommunication networks. The Internet became commercialized through privately run Internet Service Providers in the 1980s, and expanded even more by popular use in the 1990s. Since then, the Internet has had an enormous impact on the way we live and do business, mainly through the development of the World Wide Web. The Internet and the World Wide Web continue to grow and develop. Some of the Internet's major advances are increased speed, capacity and functionality.

Even more recent than the Internet, and holding a greater promise of speed and connectivity, is the Internet2. Internet2 is a consortium of many high-speed networks that are interlinked by fiber optic backbones. It enables data transmission speeds up to 2.4 gigabits per second, which is 45,000 times faster than a 56 Kbps modem, and it supports new types of applications that cannot operate over the existing Internet. Some of these applications include virtual 3-D videoconferencing, interactive television, and operation of specialized equipment such as the CyberScalpel, a virtual surgery that enables local hospitals to access resources and skills only available at larger institutions.

No longer are desktop and laptop computers the primary ways of accessing the Internet. A large number of ICT devices and systems such as phones, game consoles, and surveillance and security systems are capable of interacting with relevant services through the Internet, and the list of such devices is increasing. Already developed is an Internet-enabled refrigerator that can manage the pantry and send email to the supermarket with a shopping list and a delivery schedule.

The World Wide Web and the Internet are not the same thing. The Internet is a network of interconnected ICTs, while the World Wide Web is the set of interconnected documents and applications linked through hyperlinks and Uniform Resource Locators (URLs); The World Wide Web is a service that is enabled by the Internet. In 1990, only a few had predicted how successful the Internet and the World Wide Web would become. At present, there may be over one hundred million websites that together comprise over 30 billion web pages. Better connections and increased speed have greatly contributed to the rapid expansion of electronic commerce, videoconferencing, telecommuting and virtual environments.

Wireless telephone communications was a major advance for making interconnectivity and communications among ICT devices possible. While the first U.S. patent for a wireless telephone was issued in 1902, it took another 60 years to develop technology that resembles the current cell phone system, and hand-held cellular radio devices have been available since 1973. Mobile phone networks have spread rapidly throughout the world since then, because of their low establishment costs and rapid deployment.

The evolution of mobile telephony has spanned four distinct generations. In 1945, the zero generation (0G) mobile telephone was introduced. These phones were not much like the current cellular type, and they involved a base station covering a wide area within which each telephone would occupy a channel when used. These phones could not be transferred from the signal coverage of one base station to another, and were therefore confined to a specific area. Bell Laboratories invented cellular technology in 1984, and this involved multiple, centrally-controlled base stations (also called 'cell sites'). Each base station provided service to a small area (also called a 'cell') that was set up to overlap partially with other cells. In this way, the phone could be transferred from one cell to another without the loss of signal, and this resulted in a much greater area of operation throughout the cellular system.

The first mobile phones were large and heavy, about the size of a handbag, while technological advances have since then facilitated their miniaturization and even the integration of mobile phones into wristwatches. The first commercial cellular network was introduced by a Japanese company in 1979, and the first fully automatic 1G (first generation) cellular networks were launched in the early to mid-1980s in Northern Europe. These were followed by the development of the first digital 2G (second generation) cellular network technology in 1991 in Finland on the global system for mobile communication (GSM) standard. The launch of the 3G (third generation) cellular network technology occurred ten years later in Japan on the wideband code division Multiple Access (WCDMA) standard. The deployment of the third generation (3G) is today driven by applications such as video and TV services, and in the immediate future we will enjoy the fourth generation (4G) technology, which is characterized by a low-cost and high-speed data transfer that can enable a high degree of personalization and synchronization between various user ICT devices.

Many other ICTs and applications, and related technologies, have obviously also played crucial roles in getting us to where we are today. Examples of such are display technologies that have lead to the development of ultrathin high definition screens that can make laptops, cell phones and other devices much smaller, lighter and with boosted functionalities. Another example of an essential ingredient of better ICT devices is the ever improving battery technology, which enables the operation of laptops and other devices for long periods without the need to re-charge.

It is important to recognize that ICT may not have been a driver of change in itself, but a tool that first enabled change toward the release of creative potential and knowledge, and then spread these bursts of creativity and knowledge through societies. In other words, ICT does not by itself create transformations in civilization, but facilitates the creation and dissemination of knowledge that drives the innovative society and the knowledge economy. Wealth generation is becoming increasingly dependent on (1) the use of ICT, and (2) the capacity to add value using ICT both at a personal and corporate level. ICT will continue to evolve at a fast pace and enable current practices to be performed at greater speed and efficiency, as well as enable new practices. In the future, economic survival will require the use of ICT at a variety of levels, for individuals, for societies, and for corporations and other organizations.

For those on the road to using paperless ICT to become more efficient and live more fully, this book can assist in and prepare you for the journey to paperless joy.

3. IMPROVED QUALITY OF LIFE AND WORK – WITH PAPERLESS ICT

Have you ever felt that you have become confined, or restricted, to live at a location and according to a time schedule, that does not feel natural, because of professional reasons? Work locations, employment opportunities and real estate prices are the main factors that have driven us into this situation. Let's look at why these restrictions are so bad for us and how we can gain our freedom back through paperless joy.

In the previous chapters we have seen how important ICT has been throughout history, and how it has contributed toward great progress that led to an improvement of life quality. In the next chapters I'll introduce you to how you can use ICT to make your own leaps, both in your private and professional lives, and at a broader organizational and societal level. First, we'll look at how to use ICT toward more natural work and life rhythms, while at the same time becoming more efficient and productive. In order to embark fully and in a committed way on this journey—lifestyle transformation through paperless ICT—it is important to recognize and be convinced of the many advantages offered by ICT-based paperless work- and lifestyles. Change happens first in the mind, and then behavior change follows. While the main advantage stems from the liberation of location and time constraints on task performance, a number of other ICT-enabled paperless features add to the advantages. In Chapters 13 we will look at ICT-enabled transformations and their advantages at an organizational and business level—from the employer's and employee's perspective.

First I'll explain why it's so important to distribute tasks over time and space in a more natural way, matching our own innate biological rhythms, and to introduce variety, which provides stimulation in our work environment. Then we will look at ways to achieve this with ICT, by going paperless, being connected, being location and time flexible, and multitasking.

Most of us have, since our childhoods, become conditioned to believe that work has to be performed at the location of the employer during a specific time period of the day, while staying at home was often associated with unemployment. According to the traditional work ethics, longer working hours results in greater productivity and success. Employers often pay great attention to the actual time employees spend at the workplace, instead of focusing on employee productivity, which in most cases is not linearly correlated to the time spent in the office. In fact, a common misconception exists that the time spent in the work place is positively, and even linearly, correlated to how much work an employee produces (productivity). Employees who spend many hours in the office are therefore often viewed as more productive than those who spend less time, ever if the latter get more and higher quality work done. Why does this misconception exist? It emerged from traditional work ethics that were mainly based on highly repetitive work tasks that often required little creativity and innovation. In connection to this misconception is also the belief that the more an employee is seen at work, the more s/he is producing, and it has therefore in some work environments become more important to be seen than to be productive. The traditional workstyle has become particularly incompatible in today's knowledge and information economy, where the majority of professionals perform ICT-based analytical tasks that require a high degree of creativity and innovation. Productivity is therefore more dependent on an agile state of mind and less dependent on the amount of time spent on working. A new work philosophy —success formula— has emerged as a result of the increased competition and requirement for intellectual quality, and the shift toward a knowledge-based economy in which information and knowledge have become key commodities. What matters now are product and service innovation, quality, efficiency and speed, rather than simply quantity.

Our standards of living with regard to the quantity and quality of available goods and services, including health care, education and employment, have risen remarkably in the last 50 years. Along with this improvement, we would have expected an equally generous increase in quality of life as measured by health, diet, working and living conditions, leisure time, stresslessness and happiness. Paradoxically, this has not occurred, and instead many of us have ended up with a relatively low quality of life despite an abundance of available products and services. We find ourselves forced to live in places that don't suit us, we spend several hours a day commuting to and from a workplace that was not designed according to our likings, and we spend less time with family and friends. On top of these constraints, we are further obliged to pay a high monetary price for real estate in proximity to our offices, and we pay dearly in fuel costs for commuting. We have simply become trapped in work- and lifestyles that are incompatible with our biological human natures, living at locations, in conditions and according to time-schedules we did not choose.

A. Work with your biological clock

To some degree all of our physiological (body and mind) processes are regulated and affected by our biological rhythms, which can be likened to a clock that tells our bodies and minds when to perform activities such as sleeping, eating, exercising and even thinking. In fact, this biological clock affects not only our physical reactions, but also our mental ability and even our moods—how we feel when we wake up, how fast we can compose a work description, how quickly and accurately we can proofread a text and how well we perform in a physical exercise.

Jet lag is a good example of what happens when our activities become incompatible with our biological rhythms, when we try to force our daily activities into the wrong phase of our body clock. This natural clock is synchronized with the cycles of light and dark, and every individual seems to have his/her own unique clock settings, while some common features of human daily activity patterns have also been recognized. Hence, not all individuals have the same patterns or phases of productivity during the day, and some of us are said to be "morning persons," while others are "afternoon" or "evening persons," or "night owls." Studies have shown that our capacity to memorize varies at different times of the day. Some studies have suggested that most of us have a better short-term memory in the morning, while our long-term memory is stronger in the afternoon. Organizations may consider these findings and thus execute planning sessions that requires long-term memory in the afternoon. Since biological clock-regulated abilities are also dependent on the light cycle, they may, therefore, also be strongly affected by seasonal changes and even by the deprivation of the complete natural light spectrum that occurs as a result of inadequate office lighting. There are some general day phase settings that seem to be common for most of us. For instance, efficiency increases in the first morning hours of the working day and reaches a peak around 4 p.m., before it begins to decline.

Here is an example of how a more detailed daily productivity profile with its main phases can look:

Early morning phase (8 a.m. to 10:30 a.m.): High energy, stamina and alertness. Best phase for mentally demanding tasks such as important meetings, planning and initiating new projects and dealing with important clients. Peak performance occurs during this phase.

Late morning phase (10:30 to noon): Decreasing energy, stamina and mental alertness. It is time for a coffee break, and getting material ready for upcoming tasks, and engaging in non-urgent and less important activities.

Early afternoon phase (1 p.m. to 3:00 p.m.): Lunch has provided an energy boost and most of us may at this phase experience our peak for the day. Stamina and mental acuity is usually high and optimal for performing demanding and critical work tasks.

Mid-afternoon phase (3 p.m. to 4 p.m.): Decreased blood sugar levels lead to a loss of momentum and decreased stamina and mental alertness. A coffee break may help, but not for very long.

Late afternoon phase (4 p.m. to 7 p.m.): Energy depletion may at this phase cause a certain stress and anxiety if we still have work tasks to complete.

Dinner time phase (7 p.m. to 10 p.m.): Today's hectic pace of business often demands work even in this late phase. Peak productivity can here be maintained by taking 5-10 minute pauses to rest when the feeling of fatigue becomes too overwhelming.

Our biological clocks, also called circadian rhythms, coordinate the timing of internal bodily functions, such as sleep and our interactions with the external environment. Several studies have shown that being productive for long continuous time periods is simply not possible for most of us. Our creative and analytical abilities and performance will start to subside after only two to three hours, and it will require refreshing and replenishment via pleasant and stimulating activities in our surroundings. During an eight-hour work day, most office workers use fewer than three hours (or 35%) for active production—coined the 20/80 principle in management—which states that of the things we do during the day, only 20 percent really matter. Only 20 percent of our activities will produce 80 percent of the output product. By identifying and focusing on those things we can greatly enhance productivity and free up time that otherwise gets wasted. The non-productive five or six hours are usually spent on daydreaming, chatting with colleagues, browsing the Internet, extended coffee and lunch breaks and so on. The question is, did we really have to spend those five or six hours at work? Probably not—but because of fixed work schedules, we end up doing so.

People who suppress or ignore their daily biological rhythms and perform tasks at non-optimal hours often experience diminished productivity, sleep and digestive disturbances and other medical conditions.

Several factors determine (1) how long we can stay productive, and (2) the best ways to increase overall productivity during the course of the day. Advances in our knowledge of biological rhythms and how they regulate bodily functions and behaviors can have broad economic impact, because this knowledge can be used to prevent medical conditions and optimize business practices. The 9 to 5 work schedule may not suit everyone equally well, and many of us therefore end up having to force our daily productivity pattern to a non-productive schedule. Flexibility by which we can adapt our work schedule to our innate biologically controlled productivity pattern can therefore impact positively on our performance, health and well being. Some recent studies have in fact shown that employees who work on flex-time can experience many advantages both in terms of personal well-being and productivity. Absenteeism, lateness and employee turnover decreased significantly when flex-time work schedules were introduced and employees could decide when to perform their work tasks during the day or week. At least 50 percent of business organizations that implement flex-time have reported improvements in productivity, as well as lower stress rates for employees. This was attributed to the fact that efficiency varies during the course of the day and that individuals can vary significantly from the average peak productivity phase pattern. Another result of being able to plan the day's schedule in an independent manner, instead of being told when to do work tasks, is a feeling of empowerment that greatly contributes to stress relief and elevated stamina.

Paperless ICT is in most cases a prerequisite for the implementation of an efficient flex-time work schedule, because it allows people to perform work tasks from almost anywhere and at any time. It would simply not be possible to relocate a paper-based office between the work place, home office and our favorite café in the way we can carry around an Internet - enabled laptop. However, to make the most out of a paperless flex-time workstyle employers must allow their employees to determine their own optimally balanced work office / home office time-distribution, and not require a 8 hours per day or 35 hour per week work office location even if at a flexible time schedule.

B. Stimulate your work environment with ICT

In the earlier sections we have seen how important our state of mind is for productivity in today's knowledge economy work environment. Our analytical and creative abilities, which are essential to productivity, can rapidly subside and be overrun by fatigue if our mental energy is not replenished through positive external stimulation in our work environment. This stimulation, to a large extent, derives from elements of variation. We have all experienced routine leading to boredom and fatigue. In fact, all work tasks, including those that seem repetitive and routine-based, can improve significantly in terms of productivity and employee happiness with added environmental stimulation. Many work tasks that require out-of-the-box style thinking, where one has to reframe the situation and view it from different angles to reach innovative solutions, are particularly dependent on externally derived stimulation.

But stimulating energy- and creativity-replenishing activities are, in many cases, impossible to perform in the typical work and office environment. As a result, we become trapped in a dull situation and will succumb to a gradually increasing non-productive state. Frequently, the office environment is not one we have designed to our preferences, and it does not provide the necessary elements of quality, stimulation and variation. An interesting and pleasant environment will stimulate motivation, creativity and innovativeness, while a dull environment will lead to mental fatigue. Since "interesting" and "stimulating" are two quite subjective features, I refer to an environment which is customized to our individual needs for stimulation of a productive state of mind. It is virtually impossible to create an environment that will fulfill the creativity needs of everyone equally well. Some of us function better in a minimalistic clutter free space, while others can unleash their creativity and replenish their energy when in a lively space. Our productivity is furthermore greatly influenced by our mood, which in turn is dependent on our physical environment. An agreeable environment will greatly benefit our moods.

Writers are a good example; they often travel in order to be exposed to novel and stimulating environments that will boost creativity and imagination. Spending too much time in the same environment often clogs our minds; we tend to lose perspective and don't see the larger picture, and the world becomes small, rigid and dull. In fact, it is well-postulated that boredom, fatigue and even depression arise from a lack of external stimulations and a forced adaptation to a life rhythm that is incompatible with our nature. The introduction of variation and stimulation, in combination with a freedom to distribute work over time in a more organic fashion, can unlock a remarkable degree of productivity.

Taking all this into consideration, an obvious way to generate the external stimulation that can boost stamina and productivity is to introduce appropriate variation into our working environment by simply changing it, and this is where ICT can work wonders. Paperless ICT can enable us to perform work from almost any location, while still maintaining essential communications with employees and clients, and to have access to company information resources. Why become trapped in a dull office environment when you can unleash your productivity in your living room, on a campground, or simply at an Internet café near your work office. Paperless ICT will also make wonders for those who still need to work from the employer's office environment by reducing the distracting clutter of paper piles, file cabinets and shelves, and as such also free up space and provide a more airy work environment.

Paradoxically, however, despite the very obvious advantages of the location and time flexible workstyle, both from employees' and employers' perspectives, many of us are still confined in old-fashioned work environments. This is partly because many workers and employers may not yet have realized the full potential provided by paperless ICT, but also because of the employers' concerns that employees may not be producing when out of the control of the traditional work space. I will address these matters in Chapter 13 and demonstrate how the ICT-enabled flexible work- and lifestyle becomes a win-win situation for both employers and employees. The employee will gain in life quality, and the employer will gain in productivity and lower cost.

C. Adopt eco-friendly and energy conserving work practices

The use of ICT benefits the environment by reducing the need for paper, by curbing commuting and by decreasing the need to maintain office spaces. Those three reductions alone can greatly shrink fuel consumption and emissions.

Studies have shown that ICT contributes significantly towards increase greenhouse gas emissions. PCs, mobile phones and data centers are the main contributors, and were responsible for 2 percent of total human greenhouse gas activities in 2007—this parallels the aviation sector, which is a no trivial emissions offender. However, the same study determined that ICT would simultaneously contribute towards a reduction in emissions that is five times its own footprint. Hence, the overall result of ICT usage is largely beneficial to the environment.

The American Consumer Institute, for example, has estimated that the Internet will save the world from approximately one billion tons of carbon emissions in the next ten years. This number can be broken down into the following carbon footprint-reducing features:

- eCommerce will reduce emissions by 206 million tons of carbon, mainly in the form of reduced travel to and from stores, and store maintenance.
- ICT enables location and time flexible work (telecommuting), which will prevent 247 million tons of carbon emissions through reduced transportation.
- Reducing office construction can save 28 million tons of carbon, and 312 million tons of carbon can be saved by reducing office heating, cooling and lighting.
- Teleconferencing can prevent 200 million tons of carbon emissions if it replaces only 10 percent of face-to-face meetings over a ten year period.
- The adoption of digital newspapers could save 57 million tons of carbon.

- Replacement of first-class mail, office paper, books with email and electronic documents, and the plastics saved from music and video downloading is estimated to reduce emissions by 67.2 million tons of carbon.

A decreased use of paper will furthermore save trees and reduce the waste products created by paper production and the disposal of used paper. In sum, the overall benefits of paperless ICT to the environment are overwhelming and deserve a serious consideration in the decision for going paperless.

A lesser need to commute and to transport paper-based media, and heat, cool and maintain office spaces will also lead to great energy savings. This is a non-trivial matter in times where energy prices and supply influence national economy, international relations and how much money you have left after paying the bills.

4. KEYS TO FREEDOM

At this stage, many of you are asking the same question: How can I accomplish this ICT-enabled flexible work- and lifestyle? The answer is this: Use ICT to go paperless, be connected, be location and time flexible, and multitask. These are four integral elements of paperless joy, and they are interconnected and interdependent, and need to be applied in combination with each other for reaching the most joyful paperless experience.

A. Go paperless

In order to be able to perform tasks in a location and time independent fashion, we must be able to access, edit and distribute documents from any location and time where an ICT device can operate. Obviously, it's impossible to carry around a pile of papers and books or communicate paper documents through courier or snail mail efficiently when on the go or when working from home or some other location. In fact, the only way of having access to all your office documents in a location and time independent manner is to have them in an electronic format so that they can be stored on a hard or flash drive and be communicated through the Internet. A prerequisite for working in a completely location and time independent fashion is to become paperless and use various Internet-enabled ICT devices such as desktop and laptop computers, tablets, smartphones and eBooks to accomplish the traditional paper-based tasks. Electronic, or digitized, documents can be copied and stored at multiple locations for easy and instantaneous access, and for easy retrieval through simple searches. This allows for their access and exchange from virtually any location and time with an ICT device.

In addition to enabling a location and time independent workstyle, paperlessness can in many ways optimize various practices and make them more efficient. For instance, maintaining an electronic organizer can enable alarms to remind us of appointments and deadlines, while this is not possible with a paper-based organizer. Another advantage of paperlessness is the ease with which we can find and retrieve files; on a computer this can be done instantaneously and automatically with a search engine, while a paper in a pile has to be searched for by hand. Furthermore, digitized documents are more secure, because they can be copied and stored at multiple locations. But going paperless is not limited to scanning your documents and implementing ICT –based document editing and communications—it extends beyond that by adopting paperlessness in your interactions with all businesses such as paying bills, shopping, personal communications, and so on. Paperlessness can also enable a certain degree of multitasking which can save us from much time and also cheer up boring work tasks. We will look at this with detail in a later section.

Once paperlessness has been achieved, the possibilities for work practices linked to the knowledge economy are endless. Think of this alone: a regular 120 gigabyte laptop hard drive can store the equivalent of 5,000 books assuming an average 2 megabyte size for each. In sum, paperless practices are more efficient, more economical, can render information more secure and accessible and, finally, is environmentally responsible. Because of the central role of paperlessness in achieving a location and time independent work- and lifestyle, it will be addressed in a much greater detail in Chapter 5, and a detailed practical guide on how to go paperless is outlined in Part 2 of this book.

B. Be connected

In order to be able to perform work and other tasks in a location independent manner, we need to be able to interact with those we relate to professionally and also be able to access information. This requires connectivity to telecommunications networks and the Internet. Once connectivity has been achieved, we can be location independent in our professional and personal communications. It basically enables us to access and disseminate information, communicate and perform other tasks remotely from anywhere. ICT can enable this since it has experienced impressive developments in telecommunications applications, such as mobile telephony and wireless data, audio and video transfer. The Internet has revolutionized the way we can communicate with the rest of the world. We need ICT devices that can connect to the available Internet and telecommunications networks, access these networks through either free or subscribed services, take advantage of Internet based email and instant messenger accounts, and \ and provide remote access software that enable communications with central computers. The most important ICT communications devices are desktop computers (when working from home) and laptops with wireless capabilities, cellular phones, smart phones and wireless PDAs (when working from the road). Connection to telecommunications networks is mainly achieved through either landline-based or mobile phones, but can also be achieved through Internet-based messenger services such as Voice over Internet Protocol (VoIP). Access to the Internet can be accomplished through several routes that include telephone landlines and cellular telephone networks, wireless transfer and cable TV-based networks. These different means of connectivity are outlined in a greater detail in Chapter 17 in the second part of this book, which provides guidance on how to become paperless.

ICT users often depend on more than one type of connection or access to a network. For example, at home they may have a telephone landline-based DSL Internet access that is connected to a wireless router that enables wireless Internet access in the house and immediate surroundings; when traveling, paperless ICT users depend on a mobile phone-based connection for Internet access. The Internet access networks are undergoing rapid development, which results in a higher capacity (speed) for data transfer, and will provide functions that can better simulate direct face to face interactions.

Electronic connectivity is an essential feature for performing paperless work practices in a location and time flexible way. Advances in technology will continuously improve the ways we can communicate and exchange information in a time and space independent manner, and thus facilitate our goal to live with paperless joy.

C. Be location & time flexible

A key behavioral feature for the exploitation of paperless ICT to transform work- and lifestyles is to become location and time flexible in task performance. It's not enough to digitize office practices and documents toward a location and time independent workstyle—a change is mindset is necessary. Most of us have become conditioned and accustomed to performing work tasks from a specific location—the office—and at certain times during the day, and this habit can be deeply rooted. But ICT-based paperless practices will enable workers to free themselves from these constraints and become more flexible in their work schedules, and to perform tasks from locations and at times outside of the norm. The key is to adapt your work schedule and location to your innate biological rhythm and environment that suits you better, rather than adapting your rhythm to a work schedule and perform work from a non-productive space. We have looked at this need in the previous chapter. In this way we will perform tasks at the times and at location when and where we are most productive and get things done faster and better, thereby freeing up valuable time. By being location and time flexible, we can also use "dead time" (for instance, traveling or waiting for an appointment) to do work and thereby free up valuable time for our favorite activities. By performing a boring work task in a stimulating and pleasant environment, we can make the unpleasant task more pleasant. Adopting a location and time flexible workstyle and schedule may not be a straight forward transition, and it will therefore require some planning and practice. Furthermore, not all ICT-based tasks may be suitable for every type of location or time during the day. Initiate this important transformation now and start working from a location and at the times you feel most productive. In the next section that addresses multitasking we will also see how important it is to become location and time flexible to get things done more efficiently and pleasantly.

D. Multitask

The fact that we are not constrained by location and time in ICT-based task performance means that we can work on almost any assignment at any given time, even when we are engaged in some other activity that does not require significant attention or intellectual activity. For instance, when we are waiting for an appointment, when we commute in a train or even drive a car, we can perform various ICT-enabled tasks. This is called multitasking, because we are performing multiple tasks simultaneously. Many have advised against multitasking, citing a consequent loss of focus and thereby performance; multitasking can distract us, diminishing our focus on getting things done in the most efficient way and at the highest quality of output. This is true when incompatible types of tasks are combined for multitasking. But multitasking can boost productivity and save time when appropriate tasks are combined and performed simultaneously. It would, of course, be unwise to work simultaneously on two mentally demanding assignments that require a high degree of attention; but combining a passive activity with a more attention-demanding activity works well and will render the passive and often boring activity more pleasant.

It's incredible, the tally of how many hours are wasted every day on simply waiting, commuting and other activities that don't involve any productive activity. For example, you can drive while listening to an audio book, or wait for a doctor's appointment while working on a job task using a laptop or, if it's not rude, talking with a client on a cell phone. You can read an eBook from your smartphone while commuting by rail, or make notes on how to organize an upcoming business meeting. Clearly, certain ICT devices are more appropriate than others, depending on the type of multitasking activities. "Reading" information via an audio source is preferable when we need to have our hands free for other things and are on the move, while a light laptop is convenient when commuting or waiting for an appointment. It is also possible to write and edit texts while driving, by using a digital dictaphone that can be connected to a voice recognition software to convert the dictated words into typed text. We can also view videos on the go by using wearable video glasses in combination with a portable multimedia device or a Digital Audio Broadcasting (DAB) -enabled receiver that can pick up TV channels.

Of course, we also need time to daydream, reflect or simply do nothing, and passive but time-consuming activities such as commuting and waiting can provide the time for doing that. The goal of using passive time to accomplish work tasks through multitasking is not necessarily to get more work done, but to free up more time for your favorite or preferred activities. It is important to have clarity about your goals: Would you like to free up more time, or would you like to be more productive? Knowing the answer to this question is important, because it's easy to fall into the trap of working much more than before while multitasking with ICT.

Multitasking with ICT devices can also work wonders by cheering up otherwise dull work tasks. We often hear that we must love what we do, and, because we spend such a very large portion of our lifetime working for a living, it makes sense to make this time as agreeable as possible, even if the actual task isn't. The quantity and quality of output will increase when the time spent on work passes by pleasantly. One way of making certain job tasks more enjoyable is to blend or associate them with enjoyable activities. In this way, they will become more pleasant, because the actual time spent on them will have a pleasant constituent. Consider, for example, about how differently we experience boring and repetitive work tasks if we're listening to our favorite music, or if we're surrounded by an interesting and stimulating environment. ICT devices can be used very effectively for transforming an unpleasant work experience to a pleasant one. Computers, mp3 players and even smartphones can be used to listen to music or audiobooks while working at the same time. In fact, music has been proven in several studies to be a potent mood and creativity enhancer.

We have seen how the four essential and interdependent elements of paperless joy – paperlessness, location and time flexibility, connectivity and multitasking – can enable a new way of living which is more compatible to our own nature and provides a greater freedom in professional and private life.

5. WHY PAPERLESS IS BETTER

An essential effort during your journey toward a flexible location and time independent workstyle and to live with paperless joy is to adopt paperless practices, and I will therefore elaborate on this in a much greater detail. The terms "paperless," "electronic" and "digital" are often used interchangeably, describing a mode of work (previously done on or through paper) adapted to ICT devices (hardware) and software. To become paperless means, essentially, that the traditional paper-based practices such as writing, note-taking, reading, editing, communicating and even drawing are implemented electronically with ICT devices and software. Much has been said and written about the paperless office in recent years, and the rapid development of ICT is continuously enabling an increasing number of paperless practices.

Paradoxically, however, the consumption of paper has increased exponentially since the advent of personal computers and printers. The main reason is that we have become conditioned to use paper and may not fully grasp the various opportunities and advantages provided by digitization.

Nevertheless, the advantages of substituting paper-based practices with digital practices are numerous and I will iterate some of the most important.

A. Enable flexible work schedules and generate more free time

Digitization of paper-based office practices can lead to remarkable time-savings and flexibility in work scheduling. For example, instead of searching for a document in stack(s) of paper or retrieving it from file cabinets, it could be rapidly retrieved in seconds with the help of a search engine. In addition, digital documents can be accessed at almost all times and from nearly all locations where an ICT device can be operated. Even deeply embedded content within an electronic document or library can be identified and retrieved by a large number of users located in diverse geographic locations via the use of sophisticated search engines.

Time-savings will result from the elimination of copying, printing and exchanging paper documents through snail mail and courier. The flexibility provided by office digitization will furthermore allow for a more efficient use of unutilized "dead time," when one is, for instance, waiting for a flight, a dentist appointment, commuting on a train, or attending a meeting that has become unbearably boring. In fact, many of us waste an incredible amount of time by simply waiting. In such situations, work can be accomplished through the use ICT device(s) to read, write, edit, and communicate documents. In this way, digitization of office practices will also allow the freedom to choose the time when tasks can be done. The miniaturization of ICT devices has made this location flexibility easy to accomplish. Laptops weighing less than 2 pounds (or 0.9 kgr) can interact through the Internet through wireless connections. Electronic books the size of a paperback can hold over 400 books in their memory card. Smartphones can hold over 200 audiobooks, and they also provide Internet browsing, GPS navigation and DVD-quality video recording. This flexibility, and the time saved, can change our lifestyles and enable us to spend more time on the things we really enjoy doing, while at the same time becoming more productive.

B. Enjoy a greater freedom of mobility and a lesser need to travel

A shift towards paperless practices will allow work to be done from anywhere in the world that an ICT device can operate—essentially most locations a human being would enjoy spending more than a couple of hours. Thanks to global roaming telephony and wireless email and Internet, your office will basically follow you and be accessible everywhere. If a tablet-PC is too large or heavy to carry, a lightweight PDA or electronic book may solve the problem. Alternatively, any business office in a hotel would allow retrieval of documents or operation of your office computer, from the other side of the globe through remote access software. A high-storage capacity flash drive can allow you to carry thousands of documents in your pocket, while a portable hard drive can harbor the paperwork of an entire department.

In 2006, it was estimated that a total of 250 million people belonged to the mobile workforce, and this number is expected to drastically increase in the next decade. According to the International Data Corporation (IDC), 75-percent of the U.S. workforce will be mobile by 2012, and in Japan it will exceed 80-percent. The worldwide number of mobile workers is predicted to reach one billion by 2011. In fact, companies will be forced to mobilize a large proportion of their work force in order to maintain competitiveness in the era of globalization, and office practice digitization can therefore be viewed as a key component of corporate success. In sum, the freedom for greater mobility through office digitization can allow the office to be taken to the most pleasant places. The increased necessity for work travel and commuting, because of the global nature of the workforce and the separation of residential and work locations, can, however, also become a major and costly inconvenience at both the personal and corporate professional level. Office digitization can greatly reduce the need to travel and commute, because work can be performed at almost any location, documents can be easily exchanged across geographic locations, between your home and employer or customer, and ICT can simulate face to face interactions.

A variety of ICT-based communication systems can enable remote live communications such as audio and video conferencing. These technologies are evolving and developing at a remarkable pace, and thereby facilitating and enabling a variety of features of instant communications. Already, it's no great technical challenge to link up 10 to 20 conference participants from different parts of the world through Internet-based teleconference software and communicate interactively, while simultaneously presenting slides and video. In sum, paperless ICT can provide the flexibility to either travel and perform work tasks on the go, or to perform them from home and eliminate the need to travel.

C. Gain greater control of your private and personal business

Office digitization generally leads to a feeling of being in a greater control over professional activities, because all documents and communications can become instantly accessible and safely backed up at multiple locations. Mobile workers will not find themselves saying, "Oh, I forgot that document in my office and can't access it now," or "Where did I put that folder, I can't find it," or even worse, "Gosh, I must have trashed that pamphlet." There is a lesser need to remember the location of documents, because they easily can be retrieved with search engines. This frees up brain memory and capacity, and instead of being preoccupied with remembering where this or that document is, we can spend that brain capacity on more creative, productive and important thoughts. The capacity to copy and clone documents and store them at multiple locations leads to a greater feeling of safety, because it is now essentially impossible to lose an important file. PDA and smartphone-based organizers that can synchronize wirelessly with multiple computers adds to the feeling of control, because all of our paperless calendar appointments, task lists, notes and contact information will be accessible in a location and time independent manner, and be safe from loss. These electronic calendars will also automatically remind us of when important events and tasks are due and there is therefore a lesser chance that we would miss appointments and deadlines.

D. Save money

Based on what I've said in the previous sections, it's easy to understand that one of the many advantages of office digitization is cost saving. In addition to the cost savings and the increased profit that results from enhanced productivity, office digitization also cuts costs by decreasing the need for paper, printing, photocopying, fax, distribution, mail and courier services, office and storage space, rent, facilities expenses, commuting, traveling and, finally, personnel. It also contributes towards the implementation of green business strategies that can lead to savings through tax breaks and subsidizing. The additional cost for acquiring certain electronic devices and software to enable paperless implementation will be trivial, because most office workers already have PCs, laptops, PDAs, smartphones, and so on. It is important to integrate the paperless workstyle in a company's overall strategy to make sure that appropriate ICT components, that can enable paperlessness, are acquired. Consider how much space would be freed up by eliminating all file cabinets in an office department. Two-gigabyte hard drive space can hold information equivalent to paper documents that would require a four-drawer filing cabinet. A $50 hard drive with a capacity of 150 gigabytes has the equivalent storage capacity of 70 filing cabinets, which cost about $35,000 and need a space of about 1100 square feet (or 102 m^2).

E. Safer document archiving

Office digitization will allow for safer archiving of documents, because they can be backed up and stored at multiple geographic locations and on many servers. Documents will thereby remain much safer in case of natural and accidental disasters such as flooding and fires. Multiple levels of digital storage can also protect against accidental trashing. A variety of software solutions that exist today essentially renders the backup process automatic and will thereby not require any commitment from the user. Attention will, of course, have to be focused on the safe storage of electronic documents to avoid their access by unauthorized individuals. It will also be important to ensure conversion of files and documents from older software versions to more recent versions, as well as their transfer to new storage media and devices as they develop, before the original devices and file formats become incompatible. Chapter 17 discusses ICT security issues in a greater detail.

F. Increased productivity

Once the office has become digitized, it can be taken anywhere and not have to be confined to a certain place. This mobility will enable work to be performed on more flexible schedules, and you will not need to perform tasks during the traditional 9 to 5 period. This may be one of the most important advantages of paperless office practices, because it can greatly affect productivity and creativity. The spatial and temporal freedom can counteract fatigue, boredom and routine, and thereby enhance overall stamina, which is a key ingredient for productive and creative performance. Some people are more productive in a quiet room, while others can unleash their creativity more efficiently in a crowded café. Yet others are more productive in the morning hours, while other perform better in the evening. Working from a quiet resort on the Caribbean coast or a high-tech office in Manhattan can have quite different influences on the creativity and productivity of different people. Paperlessness enables customization and adaptation of work task performance schedules to the most optimal workstyle for each individual. Paperless processes are also many times faster than paper-based processes, because searches, retrieval, editing, communication and archiving of documents can be done more efficiently and quickly. A paperless office is also clutter free and this type of minimalistic environment is many times more conductive for maintaining a peaceful mind that facilitates a greater focus on our specific work task. Paperlessness can as such be very beneficial for getting the things that matter most done. A greater focus on the most important tasks will make us more effective and efficient in our approach to reach our goals.

G. Environment friendliness

We have already discussed the eco-friendliness of ICT based practices in Chapter 3, and here I will only mention some specific environment friendly features that directly relate to the lesser use of paper. Paper has been estimated to make up approximately 35 percent of our waste stream, while only 48 percent of the paper products we use are recycled. The rest sits in landfills or is incinerated, producing greenhouse gasses. Obviously, a reduction in paper use will conserve forests and other resources required to make paper. The production of paper in itself consumes a great deal of energy and often produces toxic or harmful waste products that contaminate soil, air and water. Transportation of paper products to offices further contributes to increased carbon emissions and energy consumption.

6. ADDRESSING CRITICS OF THE PAPERLESS OFFICE

Have you noticed how the articles, that address paperlessness in the media every once in a while, so frequently raise various obstacles towards the road to paperless joy. It is true that a paperless work-style until recently was a cumbersome endeavor, but technology has in the past decade enabled applications that can overcome these hinders and provide superior performance to paper for the most part.

Despite today's readily available ICT solutions for the digitization of paper-based applications and tasks, and the many advantages of such practices, we have not fully transitioned to a paperless workstyle, and, paradoxically, the use of paper has increased with the introduction of ITC into our work environment. Given the advantages of a paperless office, why is society not yet there? I believe that there is a persistent myth that paper is superior to ICT applications, and I'll outline and respond to this criticism later in this chapter. However, the main obstacle for the adoption of a paperless workstyle is the fact that, since our early stages of intellectual training, we have become conditioned to use paper, and this deeply rooted habit can be difficult to change without guidance and effort. Furthermore, paper has been purported to possess several advantages over digital media in that it is tangible and also that it facilitates the organization and logical structuring of work.

Social scientists have made a strong case in the favor of paper-based work practices and even named the paperless office a myth. One advantage of paper is that it's tangible and spatially flexible; it can be picked up, flipped around and read in a non-sequential manner. Paper is tailorable in that we can easily navigate and annotate it without altering the original text. One study has shown that for some paper-based work tasks, a significant amount of information that is associated with the actual paper documents is not necessarily contained in the document's text. In group settings, for instance, the physical embodiment of information on a paper page allows colleagues to gain information about how this information is perceived by the reader, simply by observing how s/he relates and treats the paper physically.

Another interesting study has shown that the seemingly disorganized paper piles that occupy messy offices do in fact have an organizational value in that they contain important information on, for instance, the priorities, history and meaning of the documents contained in these piles. As such, these stacks and their location on the desk function as complex mental maps that help us organize our thoughts and tasks.

Reading documents from a computer screen has furthermore been associated with eyestrain and lack of portability—considerable drawbacks compared to paper.

The persistence of and dramatic increase in paper use over the past 15 years is an unfortunate result of the introduction of computers and printers in the office workspace. These devices have made it too easy to create the kind of documents that only professional printers could produce in the recent past. Easy editing of documents also leads to the printing of multiple versions of the same document. The Internet provides a wealth of information and its users often print hard copies of their research findings.

Many of these pro-paper arguments are still valid and deserve a detailed consideration, while others have been made obsolete by advances in technology. In fact, it wouldn't take much effort to replace most paper-based practices with digital habits, without a significant loss in the specific functional attributes that are associated with paper.

Paper is said to be portable, cheap, safe, stable, easy to archive, and recyclable. But digital documents can provide several advantages in each of these areas. For instance, an eBook that can be carried in a coat pocket can contain the equivalent of 400 books and other documents; this type of portability and cost efficiency simply cannot be achieved with paper-based books or documents. The stability and safety of archiving is much greater for electronic documents, because they can be backed up and stored in multiple media formats and at many locations. Even acid-free paper, which is said to have a life span of about 1000 years, is still vulnerable to fire and other disasters, as well as physically bulky and heavy, rendering its long- term storage costly. Electronic documents are 100 percent recyclable, and an increasing number of ICT devices are designed to be recyclable.

Many people argue that the tangible nature of paper has its advantages. There are, however, many viable ICT substitutes. A tablet-PC, for example, is also a tangible medium that will, with time, become lighter, thinner and bendable, and will provide an unlimited writing area. Documents are easily navigable by the use of vertical and horizontal scroll bars, and finding specific sections and even words through the use of electronic bookmarks and search tools in a digital document is much easier than on paper. Notes and data can either be entered conventionally using a keyboard, or written using a stylus. One can justifiably argue that electronic documents on a tablet-PC or even on a conventional desktop computer provide much more powerful scribbling and note-taking capabilities, as an infinite number of notes and other documents of almost unlimited size, including pictures, music and video can be linked to it. Highlighting and underlining tools on tablets provide a variety of shape and color choices, and are erasable if one desires to restore the document to its original form.

Much of our paper use has traditionally been associated with reading newspapers and magazines. While these media can also be obtained in a paperless manner, through the Internet, it has been argued that paper is still superior to scrolling through the news in a sequential manner on an ICT device. Paper is said to provides a holistic view that allows the reader to wander around the page and soak up information in a single sweep. While this may be true, the ICT mediated news provides the reader with an unlimited cyber, or virtual, area. Through a computer or eBook reader, you can in seconds jump to the different pages of a news-"paper" and also have all the past issues at your fingertips. Through a simple keyword search you can retrieve all articles on a specific subject matter in seconds, and not only from one single newspaper but from several. The obstacle here is mostly of a psychological nature and has to do with how we have been conditioned to read the news, and I will discuss these in a greater detail in Chapter 16.

The messy office desk with paper piles that function as a mind map for logical storage of information can be simulated on a desktop where different documents are placed at different locations on the two-dimensional space. Currently, specific software is being developed in which the actual desktop has the appearance of a three-dimensional tabletop, and documents and files can be organized at different locations in piles. In fact, a cyber "messy" office can potentially provide much greater functionality in that it can be even more alive with a larger potential to generate associations, but it can also be easily searchable, portable, globally accessible and protect against the accidental loss.

The current difficulties with reading documents on monitors will be resolved with new monitor technologies and electronic ink paper technology that closely simulates the look of paper documents. Some other advantages of paper over ICT applications, such as legal requirements for signing certain types of documents as well as the lack of standardized formats for certain types of documents, need to be resolved by authorities rather than by ICT developers. This is, in fact, happening at a rapid pace, mainly because of the realized cost and time advantages for digital contract formats.

Inevitably, digital documents may not currently be able to compete on all fronts with paper, but they will soon provide more overall benefits to justify a transition toward office digitization. While this transition won't be effortless and will require some investment in equipment, training and changes of certain practices, the tradeoffs will dramatically outpace the potential drawbacks. The sooner we embark on utilizing this new technology, the sooner we can enjoy its advantages of increased productivity and freedom.

Finally, paper and its associated instruments such as pens, pencils and erasers are technologically static having virtually zero possibilities for improvements that would make their performance more efficient. ITC is, on the other hand, a rapidly evolving field that presents improvements in functionality on a daily basis. We can, therefore expect this technology to lead to the development of better paper substitutes in the foreseeable future, and later both hardware and software that will be far superior to paper with regard to all aspects.

It's a matter of tradeoffs

Of course paper is still, in certain conditions and situations, superior to today's ICT, and it is easy to get hung up on its advantages, stalling the switch to paperless. Furthermore, the transition to an ICT-based work- and lifestyle will require some effort, as we become accustomed to and skilled at the use of the different ICT devices. It will require some changes in work practices in which we have been conditioned to use paper. To succeed in the transition to a paperless, ICT-based workstyle, it's essential to recognize the tradeoffs, as with all choices in life. For organizations, this may be a more straight-forward process, in form of a cost-benefit analysis that will simply translate the transition to paperlessness into gradually increased profits with a measurable break-even point. The metrics for measuring the tradeoffs of this transition at the individual level are somewhat less standard, because they can vary from case to case. However, the benefits are outlined in this book—rest assured that the advantages of going paperless will largely outweigh paper-based work practices. Once the transition is complete and you have mastered the ICT-based practices, you will be able to enjoy your new freedom to access your work material and communicate information while spending time with friends and family at any place and time.

7. PROFESSIONAL AND PERSONAL GROWTH WITH PAPERLESS JOY

Have you ever felt that work and other commitments take up all your time and does therefore not allow you to go and learn a new language, how to become a professional writer or how to live a healthier life. This feeling can easily evolve into a feeling of life stagnation - a state where we have become caught in s vicious cycle that has stopped us from evolving further.

The liberation from location and time constraints in communications, media, reading books, watching movies or listening to music through paperless ICT devices opens tremendous opportunities for education, personal development and growth. One can literally now exchange cultural and other types of experiences, and absorb and assimilate knowledge, on the go, whenever and wherever an ICT device can operate. This becomes particularly useful at moments of "dead time," when we are constrained to a particular place or activity that does not require significant mental or intellectual input. When we, for instance, have to commute, wait in a queue, or perform some repetitive task, we can use that otherwise wasted time and simultaneously listen to a lecture or audiobook, read an eBook or even watch a film. This will sometimes require a certain degree of multitasking that, if not drawing on parallel intellectually demanding activities, will work well.

A wide range of educational institutions provide off-campus online degrees and non-degree training, as well as educational programs that can be attended on a significantly more cost-effective and location and time flexible fashion than traditional on-campus programs. The Internet and specialized software furthermore enable a very close simulation of classroom interactions. Software can enable live cyber classrooms in which students can interact both visually and aurally with each other and the teacher, using a headset and webcam. Lectures can be downloaded and listened to or watched at any time, for example when commuting to and from work, or waiting for an appointment. In this way, we can utilize otherwise dead time effectively and invest in ourselves through education, professional and personal development.

A wide range of interactive educational and training programs that include courses in a variety of disciplines and topics can be purchased on the Internet or at bookstores. Why not learn a language, or learn how to establish a home business, or read philosophy and history while commuting back and forth to work?

Some 3,000 years ago, the ancient Greeks realized that good health is a product of a healthy body and mind. A variety of audio- and eBook-based educational and personal development programs can provide coaching on both physical and psychological well-being, and these are readily downloadable through the Internet or can be purchased on CD in bookstores. One can nurture both mind and body with the help of interactive ICT in which the coaching is calibrated according to the feedback the ICT device or software is receiving from the user. In this way, the training or coaching becomes customized to our specific needs and conditions. Mental, emotional and spiritual training and relaxation can be done with both software and audio and video media that offers coaching on meditation, yoga, hypnosis, and improving mental abilities such as memory, logic and IQ, and so on. Other software and media can be used for physical improvements such as athletic coaching, reflex training and diets.

In sum, ICT offers a variety of opportunities to develop ourselves, both body and mind, in a location and time flexible paperless manner, and this is all part of the paperless joy.

8. PAPERLESS ICT IN PERSONAL LIFE

While ICT mainly was developed for professional practices and to accomplish work more efficiently, it has also changed the way we engage in many of our personal and social activities. We have already become dependent on many paperless ICT applications such as location flexible cellular telephony, email, online shopping, paying bills, playing games, reading news and listening to music. Implementation of paperless practices at home can also bring many advantages, in that we can bring many of our beloved home items with us wherever we travel. You can, for instance, bring your entire library, photo and movie collections, as well as get your bills paid, do shopping and monitor your home while on vacations.

The way we meet and communicate with people and the world has changed entirely with the use of ICT. You can talk with almost anyone from anywhere through a cell phone, and you can use the same device to send and receive emails, to send text messages and even to browse the Internet. We can express our ideas and exchange information paperlessly on our favorite subjects through blogs, discussion boards and other types of websites. The world has never been as small as it is today, thanks to ICT, and distance and location does not matter much when it comes to connecting and communicating with people.

ICT can also help organize our private life in an unprecedented way, because we can store all of our important documents in a safer digital format. We can pay bills, do and file our taxes, and earn income by selling used items online.

Today we can do close to all of our shopping, including groceries, online. Internet-based commerce provides unprecedented opportunities for both retailers and consumers; online, we can compare models and prices from many different brands and stores and thereby find the best deal. Online shopping also brings the worldwide marketplace to our front door, and it saves us time and cost, as we don't have to travel from one shop to the other to find what we need.

ICT has affected greatly the way we entertain ourselves, and mainly through media and games. Movies and music can be downloaded and viewed at home or on the go with portable media players. We can also make our own movies through a variety of video recording devices. A great variety of games are available in different formats for almost all interactive ICT devices such as cell phones and smartphones, desktop and laptop computers, and game consoles. Many of these games can involve up to several millions players who connect online. While the primary purpose of games is to entertain, several studies have shown that playing certain games can enhance cognitive abilities and traits such as leadership skills.

ICT can also be used to satisfy religious, spiritual and creative needs through software and the ability to communicate with various groups and communities.

Paperless ICT enables minimization in the space required for storage of documents and books, and it also minimizes the complexity of many activities and processes such as commuting, communication and sharing of documents. The use of ICT therefore leads to simplicity and reduces much of the life clutter that can distract us from more essential enterprises. A clutter free environment will eventually reflect itself on your mind and therefore help you to maintain focus and get things done more efficiently. It also renders practices more environmentally friendly, as fewer tangible products are produced, thrown away or shipped. Minimalist lifestyles and design have as some of their tenets an emphasis on reducing stress, enhancing focus, and prioritizing function. Practices that follow the minimalist fashion should be more functional, simpler, and more appealing from an aesthetic point of view. The paperless office is a good example of how ICT can be used to minimize, by freeing up office space from paper piles to create clutter-free surfaces.

Of course, it's important to pay attention to the clutter that easily can be generated in the cyber space by misplacing or poorly maintaining files. This cyber clutter is, however, less evident in the physical space, because it easily can be shuffled into a folder, and misplaced documents can still be found by search engines.

9. PAPERLESS ICT AND RELATIONSHIPS: PROCEED WITH CAUTION

Exaggeration of even the most joyful activities will lead to disaster, and this is also true for some of the practices that enable paperless joy.

The exponential growth of portable technologies (and the many applications that they enable) has created a real threat of addiction. People can become overwhelmed with ICT devices, or gadgets, and their use. ICT enables instant communications and networking with all other ICT users on the globe in a location and time independent manner, and this can, if not handled appropriately, lead to an information overflow—a continuous exposure to, or bombardment by, phone calls, emails and text messages. It's easy to fall into the trap of feeling obligated to manage and respond to all these outreaches.

ICT device overload is another type of addiction that is characterized by the urge to possess all sorts of gadgets that have to be carried around everywhere. In fact, studies have shown that ICT can become addictive in a similar fashion to alcohol and drugs. The addiction-like behaviors include a continuous checking of e-mail and text messages, browsing the Internet, making and receiving phone calls or playing games. If not treated, this behavior can rapidly lead to disasters in your personal and work relationships. Psychologists have classified ICT addiction as an impulse disorder that can have a socially detrimental impact similar to alcoholism, drug addiction and gambling. Studies have shown that up to ten percent of about 189 million Internet users have developed a dependency on ICT.

The development of an unhealthy relationship with ICT is accompanied by a variety of warning signs that should prompt the attention of both users and friends and colleagues, who should become concerned in these situations:

- When someone is using ICT-based means of communication even when face-to-face interaction would be easier and more appropriate.
- When someone can't refrain from responding to a text message or phone call even if the situation is inappropriate.
- When someone can't relax without checking email or text messages, or stop browsing the World Wide Web.

- When someone spends more time using ICT than socializing with friends and family.

ICT should be used to bring us closer to our loved ones, rather than estrange us from them. ICT is here to serve us, and not to be served.

Some experts believe that the addiction to ICT and related practices can lead to an impaired judgment and decision-making process. Others have noted that the frequent use of ICT and the wealth of information it brings us is actually beneficial and can train the brain's capacity for information processing; some studies have even shown that someone's cognitive abilities can become enhanced through ICT use.

Prioritizing is a vital skill for preventing the potential detrimental effects of communication overload. Moderation is the key to balancing any type of activity in life, and we must learn to make judgments regarding the appropriateness of ICT use. As a general rule, the use of ICT should not create boundaries between us and our cohabitants. ICT should be used to bring us closer to the rest of the world.

10. FIRST COMMITMENT, THEN FREEDOM

While ICT enables an immense degree of freedom to perform tasks in a location and time independent manner, it also opens the flood gates for procrastination. Working in exotic environments or at home on a flexible schedule, far away from our offices, clients, colleagues and supervisors requires a certain degree of discipline and commitment—the opportunities for alternative, and more pleasant, activities will be many. It might be tempting to spend allotted "work time" jogging on the beach, instead of completing those end-of month reports when at a seaside resort. It can even be difficult to stay focused on work tasks at home, where the allure of pets, movies, cooking and other relaxing activities are difficult to ignore. But submitting to these temptations at the expense of productivity will lead to procrastination and soon thwart advantages to be gained by ICT-enabled freedom and flexibility.

Don't let the promise of paperless joy become a curse. Realistic planning is essential to your being able to complete assignments or projects in advance of the deadline: you will need to be able to estimate accurately the time required for tasks, and you will need to stick to your schedule.

In sum: The biggest risk when adopting ICT-based work practices is procrastination, and pleasant work environments provide fertile ground for it. Procrastination has been defined as a tendency to engage in unnecessary activities to avoid doing the necessary. When a task is either boring or demanding, we may procrastinate by doing a variety of alternative activities—anything except the work we're supposed to do, even if that work is our bread-and-butter. In part two, Chapter 18, I will outline specific measures one can take to stay on the time schedule while enjoying ICT enabled freedom.

11. PAPERLESS EDUCATION

We have seen in previous chapters how ICT has transformed the way we can generate and disseminate information and knowledge throughout history and our first committed contact with information and knowledge happens during education. Educational institutions are particularly paper-intensive, and paperless practices there can not only greatly reduce paper consumption, but, more importantly, they can produce a paperless generation of students who are acculturated to using ICT-based media instead of paper. The education system is often our first contact with document generation and reading, and exposure to paperless practices at this early stage could very effectively lead to the adoption of paperlessness for life. It is in our youth that we are most receptive to learning and that we acquire most of our lifelong skills and habits. Furthermore, a paperless way of reading, researching and completing assignments would provide all the flexibilities mentioned in this book to both students and teachers. They—students and teachers—would be able to perform their school tasks at any place and at any time, and to communicate and collaborate on these tasks easily over long distances in a time-independent manner. But paperlessness goes beyond the reading, research and homework assignments. Taking exams and correcting and scoring exams, in addition to the teacher's administrative work, would become much more effective when done in a paperless manner. In fact, students and educational institutions have already begun to go paperless. Most college students do most of their work on laptops, and much of their administrative work and interpersonal interactions are done through ICT.

Educational institutions can enjoy the same cost savings as businesses and individuals by going paperless. The cost of copying and printing alone is a significant burden for schools. One could argue that laptops for each student is also expensive—but what if providing laptops to students would abolish all costs related to paper, pens, and even books, plus provide a window to unlimited information and potential for learning through the Internet? Considering the long-term gains for society, businesses and the individual, providing laptops to students would represent a rather small investment. And already we've begun to see that students of financial means not only use but depend on their laptops, regardless of whether the school is operating in a paperless manner or not.

A paperless mode of working in education will also greatly facilitate online education, which is becoming increasingly prominent and is an effective way to provide education to a much larger fraction of society at a lower cost, compared to the traditional on-site programs. Online education programs are already flourishing, and the media for delivering and assessing knowledge and experience are becoming increasingly sophisticated, to the point that some of them are surpassing traditional classroom teaching.

Paperless joy can perhaps make the most profound impact on education by facilitating the spread of, access to and assimilation of free knowledge at a global scale, without the limitations of time, location and financial burden.

12. PAPERLESS TELECOMMUTING & VIRTUAL, DISPERSED TEAMS

Much has been said and written about telecommuting in the past decades, and the number of people who work from home has increased dramatically, and will continue to increase, because of the trends outlined earlier. A telecommuter replaces his/her daily commute to the workplace with electronic communication, through the phone and Internet. While many telecommuters have dedicated home offices from which they perform work tasks, some telecommuters, called nomad workers, perform work tasks from any number of locations such as cafés, bookstores and libraries.

While telecommuting has been promoted by many organizations and enterprises, it is also associated with some disadvantages, both for the employer and the employee. To some degree, these criticisms have hampered the implementation of telecommuting programs. But these points of disadvantage, in many cases, can be resolved through paperless practices with ICT devices and software. Going paperless will facilitate many aspects of telecommuting, and I will address some of these here.

Telecommuters often find themselves isolated, because they lack face–to-face interaction with colleagues, supervisors and clients. And this dearth of personal interactions with colleagues can even lead to a lack of loyalty toward employers and colleagues.

When telecommuting is done in a paper-based fashion, the telecommuter still ends up confined to a location, with limited mobility and complicated practices regarding the access, distribution and sharing of documents and work files. A paperless workstyle that enables total mobility of the office, however, will allow workers to more easily arrange and engage in personal, face-to-face interactions with others. A paperless workstyle can deliver telecommuters from the boundaries of their home office, and allow for the occasional nomadic workstyle that will bring them into contact with colleagues or simply other people, instead of being isolated at their homes. A paperless office can also enable the telecommuter to occasionally use the employer's leased or rented office facilities to interact in a more direct way with colleagues and supervisors.

To develop and maintain friendships with colleagues and supervisors while telecommuting, an employee or employer can ritualize routines in which co-workers engage in daily chat sessions, or have their cyber-coffee together at specific pre-arranged times. Another bonding mechanism might be for colleagues to interact in a more informal manner by playing stimulating games with each other through the Internet.

One of the reasons that face-to-face communication is so important is that a large proportion of communications taking place between two or more individuals is conveyed by nonverbal means such as body language, facial expressions, eye contact and tone of voice. The information conveyed through these types of communication will obviously become compromised through a phone, or even a regular webcam. In Chapter 17 we will look at specific measures one can take to increase the communication potential through ICT, and close mimic face-to-face interactions.

Virtual teams, also called Geographically Dispersed Teams (GDT), consist of people who work together across time, space and even organizational boundaries, through ICT. A member of a virtual team is not necessarily synonymous with a teleworker, though, for a couple of reasons: (1) that team member may not exclusively work from home, and (2) virtual teams frequently consist of employees who work both from home but also in smaller groups in offices at different geographic locations. Virtual teams enable hiring and retainment of talent regardless of location. It is obvious how paperless work practices can greatly facilitate the operations of dispersed, or virtual, work teams. Because they rely on electronic communication, they can greatly benefit from paperless practices in document sharing and mobility.

13. PAPERLESS PROS AND CONS FOR ORGANIZATIONS AND BUSINESSES

In the previous Chapters I have mainly addressed the implementation and advantages of paperless ICT –based practices for the individual user and how it can enable location and time flexible work- and lifestyles, while in this chapter we will examine the profound advantages ICT can bring to organizations and businesses. This is important, because most of us earn a living as employees of small to large businesses and other types of organizations, and we can in most cases only exploit the paperless ICT-enabled possibilities described in this book to the fullest if this is compatible with the workstyle and operations of our employer. The good news is that the employer can in most cases enjoy the most profound advantages of a paperless ICT work force, and we have reached this condition through the following intertwined trends that are changing the rules of business and global competitiveness.

- Globalization, which will render the markets and products global. Competition between firms has extended from their nearest rivals to the international level. Mobility and global operations have therefore become necessary ingredient of most businesses. Competition for talent along with an increasing turnover rate among associates also contributes to the necessity for global location flexible hiring capabilities.

- The domination of information and knowledge-based production. To better illustrate this, consider that 70 percent of the work force in developed economies are information workers and even a large proportion of factory workers today make more use of their intellectual abilities than their hands. The rules and practices that determine the success of individuals and corporations are changing. In this interconnected globalized economy, expertise, intellectual property and know-how have become equally or more critical than the traditional economic resources such as natural resources, land and manpower. Knowledge-based work involves research and the generation and dissemination of documents rather than tangible products.

- The development and availability of affordable ICT and computer networking and connectivity, which enable the Internet and World Wide Web to support the exchange of information services and products.

- The increased cost of commercial and private real estate in urban centers.

- Government regulations relating to employment of persons with disabilities and environmentally responsible practices.

The use of paperless ICT is totally compatible with these trends, and one of ICT's most important attributes is that it can allow for a distributed workstyle. Distributed work has been defined to entail the conduct of organizational tasks in places that extend beyond the confines of traditional offices. It can refer to organizational arrangements that permit or require workers to perform work more effectively at any appropriate location, such as their homes and customers' sites, through the application of ICT. Going paperless is an integral part in the adoption of a distributed workstyle, because it enables time and space flexibility and total office mobility.

Organizations and companies that adapt to these new socioeconomic conditions by embracing paperless ICT to perform organizational tasks in a distributed work fashion will enjoy increased competitiveness and, finally, survival in an increasingly volatile economic environment. In order to transition and embark on the new trajectory powered by ICT-enabled paperless operations, it is important for both employers and employees to recognize the immense gains that this new route will bring.

A. Paperless telecommuting and dispersed workstyle advantages for employers

Overall, the greatest benefits that paperless ICT-based operations can offer will only be realized when employees work on a location and time flexible plan, and include:

Cost savings. Implementing distributed workstyles can gain organizations and companies significant savings such as those associated with the cost of real estate, labor and overhead that involves lighting, heating, maintenance, employee parking and so on. With ICT, work can be carried out whenever and wherever the necessary skills are available at an optimum mix of costs and other factors. Organizational growth can take place without the creation of new office space infrastructure, and the capital can instead be used to attract the best talents. For instance, companies can instead spend their funds on subsidizing housing and on salary increases.

The reduced commuting time of employees also leads to savings when transportation is in some way subsidized by the company. Other cost savings can emerge from various government incentives that encourage businesses and people to implement telecommuting, which can reduce the demand for new highways and bridges, reduce air pollution and also enable employment of disabled people. Cost savings will also result from decreased staff turnover (attrition) rates and reduced absenteeism through a total "flexible working" strategy. A healthier work force as a result of a better balance between employee work and family lives and lesser stress and exposure to the danger of traffic accidents and urban air pollution will also reduce costs in terms of health care benefits and absenteeism.

Increased productivity. Several studies have shown dramatic increases in productivity when companies implement distributed work and telecommuting strategies. Some cases have reported productivity increases up to 40 percent, while 10 to 30 percent may be more typical. Employees are not limited to working from home, but can perform tasks from different locations such as hotels, airports or client sites, and this will inevitably result in increased productive time. The location and location flexibility which allows for performance of work tasks at more stimulating environments than the traditional office cubicle will also stimulate employees to be more motivated, creative and productive and display a higher morale, and consequently less absenteeism. The abolishment of commuting time and reduced distractions that often are associated with traveling, as well as activities in a conventional workplace environment will also greatly contribute to elevated productivity. Increased productivity also results from a healthier and more motivated workforce.

Organizational and staffing flexibility. By adopting a distributed work strategy, organizations can greatly enhance their recruiting capabilities, because they are not limited to hiring employees in a specific geographic area. They can instead recruit top candidates from anywhere in the world. Distributed work strategies generally increase recruitment options and can enable rapid access to additional labor pools to meet skill shortages and allow the hire of people who need to, for whatever reason, live close to home. Companies can recruit talents across borders without costly visa application processes. Employees who would leave a company because of relocations to more attractive places or for family reasons can now remain in the work force. Employees can enjoy career breaks for studies or other reasons and at the same time continue working part-time. Employees who are on maternity or sick leave can continue performing work tasks according to their capabilities and remain up to date with the business and its practices, thereby requiring less "ramp-up" time upon returning to full-time work. A distributed work strategy also enables staffing flexibilities when organizations restructure or merge. Employers can easily restructure or reassemble working teams, as the needs of the organization change with little disruption to the company's overall operations. Teams comprising the best experience and skills for a particular task or project can be assembled, regardless of geography and time zones, and with a minimal need for travel. This flexibility can provide significant competitive advantages to corporations that need to establish presence rapidly in emerging markets in different geographic locations. Finally, a distributed work strategy can enable staff to be on standby when necessary and work on flexible hours to better match peak workloads.

Organizational resilience. A dispersed workstyle will render organizations more resistant to operational disruptions that are caused by external anomalies such as political instability, strikes, severe weather or natural disasters.

Enhanced customer service. ICT- enabled dispersed workstyles can lead to great improvements in customer services, because they can be extended beyond the workday or workweek without the burden of overtime payments. Employees with different work schedules or living in different time zones can be combined to provide 24 hour service coverage.

Improved public image. The public has become particularly sensitive when it comes to the impact of corporate operations on the environment.

A dispersed workstyle can lead to significantly reduced traffic and energy consumption and emissions created by commuting automobiles and office heating, cooling, and lighting. These environmentally responsible practices, along with the hire of homebound individuals such as the disabled or at-home parents, can only improve a company's public image, and thereby offset some of the negative impact other industrial operations may have.

B. Paperless office advantages for employers when location flexibility is not possible

While dispersed workstyles are to a very high degree dependent on paperless practices, companies that for different reasons still need to perform work in an office environment can also gain many advantages of going paperless, as can their employees.

In today's business environment, electronic paperless management can have a huge impact on process efficiency in terms of speed, dynamics, and hence competitiveness and profits.

A major paperless advantage for companies has to do with a more efficient and easy management of operations when business units and departments are dispersed over different locations. The same documents are often used by several sections that may be physically separated and may even use independent filing systems. This will require copying, distribution and filing of paper-based documents. The tedious and slow process of passing around hard copies also increases the chance of losing them or enabling their access to unauthorized entities. It is easy to see how document digitization and electronic management based on a centralized networked system can facilitate such practices in which a file can be stored in a central database that is accessible by all entities of the company and thereby becomes available to everyone who needs it at any time and from any location. Integration of Internet-enabled web-based systems can allow document access from anywhere that Internet is available, as can document sharing with third parties. This can be a particularly important feature when documents with vital information need to be made accessible instantly. Rapid access of specific documents is a major advantage of corporate paperlessness considering the time it can take to search a filing cabinet that contains hundreds of documents. A paperless electronic filing system will only require a quick search with title or keywords and the document will appear on the screen.

Besides the easier distribution, access, and filing of electronic documents, companies will also save space by scanning their documents and implementing paperless practices. File cabinets currently occupy a vast amount of expensive real estate space in companies, in addition to the cost of the cabinets themselves.

C. Benefits for employees

In order for an organization to implement an ICT-enabled paperless workstyle it is important to gain acceptance from employees. By helping employees realize how they stand to benefit from a total flexible workstyle or even the office based paperless workstyle, organizations can foster approval of this new culture. Although we already have addressed the major benefits that a paperless flexible work- and lifestyle can bring, I will recap some of the most important briefly.

More free time, reduced commuting and cost savings. These advantages may be the most attractive and represent the primary motivation to convert into a flexible work- and lifestyle through ICT-enabled work practices.

Location and time flexibility. This benefit allows for a more organic, or natural, lifestyle in which we can adapt our work schedule to our innate biological rhythms. Those who are most productive and creative in the morning hours can work during the early hours, while those who are more energetic later in the day and at night can get work done then. By going paperless, there is no need to live where the work is; we can now live where living conditions are the best for us.

Increased balance between work and private life. Even if we spend more overall hours on work tasks, we can still expect to spend more time with family and friends, and can more easily engage in home activities such as taking care of children, shopping and community work.

Better and more work opportunities. Because work tasks can be performed from any location, employment opportunities are not confined to locations within commuting distance. By perfecting the art of office digitization and developing the ability to present this in a convincing manner to prospective employers, you can significantly increase employment opportunities.

A clutter free work environment. A paperless workstyle will also result in a clutter free work environment by eliminating paper stacks, post-it notes and file cabinets. This can counteract distractions and facilitate a greater focus on specific work tasks, to get things done more effectively.

D. Benefits to society

Paperless ICT-enabled workstyles will benefit not only employers and employees, but society as a whole, and this becomes an important consideration when organizations and individuals will need to gain approval and recognition for embarking on such operational changes. The main benefits relate to reduced traffic congestions and lesser need to expand highway systems, reduced emissions and pollution, decentralization from the large metropolitan areas and a more dynamic and flexible workforce that can result in decreased unemployment. A larger proportion of disabled people can be employed on a normal working schedule and single parents who need to take care of their children at home can now enjoy the same careers as everyone else. Finally, the greater productivity of companies will finally result in a general national economic boost.

E. Considerations for the implementation of paperless location and time flexible work strategies

While the advantages are many for a paperless ICT-enabled dispersed work- and lifestyle, there are also potential obstacles and challenges that need to be considered.

One potential problem relates to performance outside the office where many other alternative and potentially more pleasant activities can detract from the focus and attention needed for work. Self-disciplined and commitment are required to stay on course with getting work tasks done in time. This has been discussed in some detail in Chapter 10. Supervisors and managers can also play an important role in helping employees be productive out of office by incorporating accountability measures and organizing the work in a way that will create self-motivating and self-driven team dynamics through interactions and collaborations between team members. By building in accountability measures in the work flow, progress is reported either directly or through email messages to enable review of accomplishments. A prerequisite for making it possible to engage in an accountability interaction with a manager is to make sure the employee is easily accessible. It is important that everyone in the working team can reach each other at almost any given time, even if they don't have to know your exact location. To implement effective reporting systems and accountability measures that can gauge and ensure work progress, companies must provide the necessary ICT and information securities, and establish appropriate policies and guidelines on what is expected from employees.

Another potential problem when working out of office is a feeling of isolation and fear that the lack of physical presence and visibility in the work place will compromise performance assessments and promotions. It is important that managers recognize the contributions by out of office workers and focus on the quality and quantity of their output rather than physical presence. In general, workers should be evaluated by their deliverables and not simply by someone watching them, because there is no guarantee that watching someone work will result in high quality work output. This becomes an easy realization if you consider that the productivity of an employee is not linearly related to the amount of time s/he spends at work, but can only be measured as the total output of work (product) produced divided by the cost, which includes salary and benefits, office space, equipment and administrative support.

Those who perform work on a location and time flexible schedule can also enhance their cyber visibility and presence by frequent communication through email, videoconferencing and telephone. Most obstacles relating to the lack of visibility and feeling of isolation can be prevented and resolved by developing policies and providing training for managers who oversee remote workers on these issues. I have also discussed some of these issues in Chapters 10 and 18. Finally, it is essential to maintain frequent contact between supervisors and employees. Electronic mail and the telephone are the primary ICT for maintaining communications. These ICT are changing at a rapid pace and will make communications more efficient, easier and realistic in the near future.

Another potential problem for out of office workers are distractions that mainly relate to the environment, such as family. It may therefore sometimes be necessary to separate work from other activities in both space and time, by even creating physical boundaries between work and other activities.

Another challenge is to maintain information and keep files secure from unauthorized access and accidental loss. Working out of the traditional office environment does increase the chance that confidential information will be compromised. A variety of security measures can be adopted by the company's information technology department to prevent such mishaps. Practical aspects of such security issues will be discussed in Chapter 17.

F. ICT and paperless practices in manufacturing-based work

While ICT-enabled paperless practices have very obvious benefits for office-based work, these practices can also be applied very successfully in manufacturing-based activities, and a variety of ICT-based practices are used to improve communication and boost productivity on the assembly lines. An increasing number of manufacturers are, for example, already implementing paperless ways to provide work instructions via electronic manuals that are displayed on flat-panel display monitors on the plant floor. The main benefit of going paperless is that it enables standardizations that in turn make the process leaner; centrally-controlled documents ensure consistency in practice, and revisions to assembly instructions can be made in seconds. Paperlessness makes it easier to update work instructions in all manufacturing stations simultaneously. By eliminating the need to sort through multiple manual instructions pages, the probability of installing the wrong part or miss a required part is minimized. It saves time, eliminates paper waste and the risk of mistranslating essential information because of manual mistakes in writing the instructions.

Assembly floor operators can use the internal web through terminals to communicate with other operators, engineers and support staff in real-time, and they can retrieve various types of information such as company performance. Quality reports can be produced and disseminated throughout the unit instantly and production can be calibrated according to inventory and sales in real time.

A seamless integration of production processes with quality control systems can allow timely identification and prevention of product defects. An interesting application in the near future may be tele-production, in which processes on the assembly floor are operated from distant geographical locations. In this case, production operators can enjoy a similar degree of location independent work- and lifestyles as paperless office workers.

While cost may be considered the most substantial drawback, the initial burden of investment and set up is only temporary and is expected to be offset rapidly through the resulting increased productivity.

14. GLOBAL DEVELOPMENT AND HEALTH THROUGH PAPERLESS ICT

While much of the content in this book may be directed predominantly towards knowledge economy workers in the developed world, paperless ICT has much to offer to the less developed and poorer societies. In fact, some of the most dramatic growths in wireless telephone communication systems, and associated applications, have occurred in parts of the world where landlines have been non-existent.

Cellular networks can now reach over 80 percent of the world's population, and 68 percent of all cell phone subscriptions worldwide were, by the end of 2006, in developing countries. More than one in ten people own a mobile phone worldwide. This remarkable expansion in the developing world can be further exemplified by the following statistics and provides an unprecedented opportunity for economic and social development:

- At least 22 percent of the Vietnamese population owns a cell phone.
- Over 4 million people in the Philippines conduct online transactions using their cell phones.
- In Afghanistan there are 20,000 fixed-line telephones and over 2 million cell phone subscribers.
- The developing world experienced a 1.4 billion increase in cell phone subscriptions at the end of 2005, compared to only 800,000 in developed countries.

The speed by which ICT devices are disseminated and diffused in developing countries is largely attributed to the highly cost-effective nature of mobile telephony and the abandonment, by the citizens, of government-run telecom systems. Fixed-line telephone networks are costly to build and maintain, and will only be profitable when customers with permanent addresses and the ability to pay the bill subscribe to them. Another problem with fixed telephone lines is that it often takes several years to get them installed and at a high fee. In contrast, mobile networks can be quickly installed in areas that have no previous infrastructure. The phenomenon of pre-paid phone cards has further boosted the spread of cell phones. Millions of users who would not normally have the ability to acquire a telephony service subscription have, through the pre-paid services, become cell phone users.

This expansion in cell phone usage provides an incredible opportunity for economic and social development, both by the virtue of enabling communication in a cost effective and paperless location and time independent manner, and by the fact that cell phones can also be used for other businesses such as money transfers and payments. Several international development agencies and economists now claim that cell phones can greatly facilitate the socioeconomic development and restructuring of developing countries, by boosting business transactions and facilitate communications that are of social and public health importance.

Major benefits that cell phones can bring to an individual, a village and a small business are:

- Earned revenue by selling phone services on a per use basis and pre-paid phone cards by individual entrepreneurs and small businesses.
- Mobile phone users can connect with the rest of the country and world and thereby gain employment and business opportunities without the need to communicate through costly and uncertain paper-based snail mail systems.
- Significant savings can be made on transportation time and costs for people living in rural communities that traditionally require travel to and from businesses.
- Information on techniques to boost crop yield, improve house construction, or teach parents how to safeguard their children's health can be provided.
- Health care workers can use mobile telephony to coordinate the prevention of disease transmission, and to coordinate emergency response in rural areas.

Here are some statistics on how mobile telephony alone has benefitted individuals and small businesses:

- As much as 85 percent of the citizens in Tanzania and 79 percent in South Africa have improved their relationships with families and friends due to cell phones.
- Profit increases as a result of cell phones have been reported by 62 percent of small businesses in South Africa and 59 percent in Egypt.

The benefits of mobile telephony also occur at the national level. For instance, cell phone penetration has been associated with higher rates of economic growth in developing countries. A developing country that has an average of 10 or more cell phones per 100 people between 1996 and 2003 would have a predicted per capita GDP growth of 0.59 percent higher than an identical country lacking mobile telephony.

In fact, some of the strongest proponents of cell phone usage in the developing world believe that economic growth should be encouraged through commerce, or "inclusive capitalism," rather than simply through the provision of international aid to enable short-term solutions. The root of all social, political and health problems in the developing world are their poor economies and lack of development. Direct monetary aid will often only result in misallocation of resources through corruption and bureaucracy, in addition to fostering dependency at the expense of self-sustainability. Support of microenterprises is more likely to stimulate healthy and sustainable development, and ICT can play a very important role in this.

Cell phones can provide the means for bottom-up economic development by, for example, allowing a farmer to grow his/her business, which in turn provides her/him with more resources to educate, feed and clothe his/her family. This type of aid has been argued to more efficiently provide sustainability, in contrast to the traditional top-down approaches that rely on aid money passed through a bureaucratic filter before reaching the beneficiaries, who in some cases become passive and dependent recipients. The connectivity of ICT is what provides the most important opportunities.

There are many classic examples from Bangladesh, India, Uganda and other developing countries that illustrate how cell phones in combination with financing and loan opportunities have opened the way for sustainable development. Public health workers in South Africa use text messaging to remind tuberculosis patients to take their medication, and in Kenya short message services (SMS) is used by people to ask anonymous questions about culturally taboo subjects such as contraception and family planning, HIV/AIDS and other diseases at no charge.

Cell phones can be used for paperless connectivity beyond the voice, as with mobile Internet, which eliminates the need for a computer to access the World Wide Web. Computers are quite rare in much of the developing world, mainly because of their higher cost, power consumption, and because an Internet connection would require wire-line infrastructure. Mobile Internet can enable people in developing countries to engage in the so-called m-commerce, to purchase goods and services using a cell phone that can function as a mobile wallet with Internet purchases deducted from pre-paid card balances.

Internet-connected computers are also becoming more common and their penetration in the societies of the developing world is expected to follow a similar trend to mobile telephony. This development will provide unprecedented opportunities in all areas that we have addressed in this chapter, plus a number of additional features, such as education through online courses and training programs. Voice recognition and text to speech applications can also be extremely useful in countries with high levels of illiteracy to provide access to knowledge to those who were denied education. While our physical world may comprise many obstacles and constraints for free and flexible moving, the cyber world can enable paperless access of the poorer populations to insights and information and knowledge that previously was only accessible to the relatively few and fortunate of the developed world. In addition, the Internet can also make the voices of the developing world heard throughout the world without constraints. To better illustrate the magnitude of the importance of ICT for the developing world in the future, consider this: the United Nations has predicted that one-quarter of the earth's population will live in slums by the year 2020. Access to the Internet through a variety of ICT devices can then provide extremely beneficial opportunities for as much as 25 percent of the worlds' population, such as access to education, expertise and business opportunities. Computers and even primitive tele-conferencing systems, in schools, can enable access to state-of-the-art lectures given in the developed world. Paperless systems in various public services agencies will also counteract bureaucracy as well as corruption since various control measures can be integrated into ICT -based office systems and a greater transparency can be achieved by making data accessible to various entities. Studies in India have shown that Internet connectivity can provide significant opportunities for improving living standards of the poor population by providing them with access to essential information regarding crop prices, weather forecasts and preventive measures to avoid infections. Another example of how Internet can help boost development is Vietnam were there was an estimated 15 million Internet users in 2007. This represents 17.5 percent of Vietnam's population and the number is expected to increase to 30 million by 2010. The country's incredible growth rate of 7,356.8 percent since 2000 has been partly attributed to the Internet which in 2000 had only 200,000 users.

In sum: mobile telephony has already transformed socioeconomic conditions and prospects in the developing world. The Internet is likely to have the most profound impact on the poorer developing world by providing its inhabitants with unprecedented means to enjoy the paperless efficiencies, services and opportunities that have been mostly restricted to the richer in the developed world.

15. BECOME A DIGITAL LIFE ARTIST

The use of ICT-enabled paperless practices to achieve a location and time flexible work- and lifestyle is not a method or procedure, but a philosophy, a way of life. A digital life artist is someone who has made his/her living an art, through seamless integration and use of ICT-enabled paperless practices that allow him/her to live and earn a living in a more natural and location and time flexible manner. A digital life artist uses otherwise wasted time to get work done and thereby saves valuable time for the activities s/he enjoys most. A digital life artist uses ICT to become more productive without working more, but spending less time on work-related activities. A digital life artist understands the importance and influence of his/her environment on his/her performance and well-being and therefore chooses his/her living and working environment according to his/her likings and not because of proximity to work. A digital life artist adapts his/her work schedule to his/her biological rhythm and life, and not vice versa. A digital life artist is environmentally responsible and heeds the call to conserve natural resources. A digital life artist sees the entire planet as his/her neighborhood and operates in a world without borders, and does not discriminate based on distance or location. A digital life artist calibrates his/her use of ICT to necessity and uses ICT to serve her/him, and not vice versa. A digital life artist is humane and does not use ICT to interact with people when face-to-face interaction is feasible. A digital life artist is aware of etiquette when s/he uses ICT and does not let it impair her/his relationships with other people or him/herself.

My hope is that Part 1 of this book has convinced you that it is possible to improve quality of life through proper use of ICT – enabled paperless practices in almost all facets of life. Part 2 provides the necessary steps and knowledge about how to become a digital life artist with paperless joy.

PART TWO
PRACTICAL IMPLEMENTATION

INTRODUCTION TO PART TWO

After reading Part I and experiencing first-hand the limitations of a paper-based office, you've probably developed the necessary motivation and drive to tackle the practical implementations. In Part II, I will introduce you to the practical approaches of becoming paperless, and how to use these new work practices in your location and time flexible work- and lifestyle. Also, I'll introduce you to methods for using ICT for presentations, conferences and private conversations. We do not all have the same level of ICT needs, nor are all ICT devices and software equally appropriate for all of our applications. While an overwhelming number of different ICT devices and software are available on the market, I will in this book remain neutral, abstaining from references to specific brands and models: I would not want to prejudice anyone toward specific systems, and I would not want this guide to be rendered out-of-date by the rapid pace of ICT device and software development. Therefore, I will refer to ICT devices and software in generic terms, outline their main features and provide guidance on how to identify the optimal components for a system perfectly adapted your specific needs. I will in this way steer you towards designing your own harmonic ICT ecosystem. However, since guidance on specific devices and software will be very useful and time saving in your quest to become paperless, I provide some information on specific systems and applications on my blog at http://enjoypaperless.blogspot.com/. In this way you can obtain the most up to date information and guidance on available ICT and where to acquire these. Customized guidance on the implementation of appropriate paperless ICT systems can also be obtained from www.digitallifeartist.com.

16. ADOPT & SUSTAIN PAPERLESS PRACTICES

A. Conditioning of paperless habits

The process of becoming paperless, as with every change process, always starts in the mind. Once we accept something as necessary and know that it will benefit us then the time is right to initiate the change process. The first and most fundamental step toward effective adoption of paperlessness or digitized practices is to become motivated, enthusiastic and positively inclined toward these. We can do this by convincing ourselves of its benefits, at both the professional and personal levels. This is particularly relevant when implementing paperless work practices at an organizational scale, where both top-down and bottom-up buy-in is critical for success; if employees are not convinced of advantages of paperlessness, the effort will result in resistance and potential failure. The change process can be successful if undertaken by reading the relevant chapters of this book in conjunction with mental preparation to become deeply, positively inclined and enthusiastic toward paperless practices and work- and lifestyle.

Changes in attitudes and practices are more effectively implemented when driven from internal desires and motivations, and we can use a variety of methods to create such states of mind. It's possible to create internal positive association with paperless practices by visualizing and imagining yourself enjoying the many benefits of paperlessness, such as the freedom of time and space, the free time for recreational activities, the un-clotting of workspace, the cost advantage, increased productivity, and finally the opportunities for personal growth. We can visualize ourselves using a tablet-PC for note taking, reading or editing texts on a LCD monitor, and generating written documents through voice recognition software. These visualization techniques work best when applied right before sleep, which allows the unconscious mind to process and prepare us for the task. You might want to imagine yourself in a pleasant location outside your regular work space, working effortlessly on a task through an office digitization device; feel how easy it is to read and take notes on a PDF document through a tablet-PC for 10 to 15 minutes before going to sleep. Affirmations can be used to enhance these visualization practices toward paperless practice conditioning. You can, for instance, say to yourself each night before going to sleep: "I am mastering the use of (insert here the specific device or software) to effortlessly create (or read) (enter here the type of document you intend to use the office digitization practice for)". Another powerful affirmation is the following: "I am mastering and excelling in the use of office digitization practices to get my all work done more efficiently. This allows me to have more free time for recreation and fun." These affirmations, in combination with visualizations, function in a similar way to a prayer and can directly access your subconscious mind to produce deep changes in your belief subsystems and prepare your conscious mind for mastering new tasks and techniques. The effectiveness of these strategies have been proven over centuries and are currently used by variety of organizations and people to master and excel in specifically demanding tasks and practices such as sports and special operations.

I will here reiterate some of the major paperless benefits that can be used in such exercises:

- Get work done in less time
- Gain greater control of your professional and personal life
- End commuting and traffic jams
- Lower your living costs
- Live where you want
- Render yourself and your organization more agile and competitive

However, the most difficult part may be to sustain this process of change, especially when the desired shift is one that radically changes the way we've become conditioned to doing things since were children. Most of us were introduced to paper-based "picture books" and paper and pens soon after birth, and the use of paper-based reading, writing and drawing practices have become deeply rooted in our habits throughout our lives; during education, personal life and later at work. Our notions about how we conceive and view documents has become strongly biased toward paper, while in a paperless world information is no longer kept in a physical file or folder, but in a software folder in a directory. The documents can't be physically handled in the same way as with paper. Reading texts from a monitor screen—even if it aesthetically mimics real paper—can feel awkward. These obstacles are of a conceptual nature and are mostly manifested at the psychological level, because paper-based practices have been deeply rooted in our belief systems. This is what is called conditioning, or learning, by doing or practice; you have done something so many times that it has become a natural practice, or habit, which is difficult to change. Conditioning is a cognitive process by which we acquire a skill. In fact, one of the most common reasons that people fail at the implementation of paperless work practices is the initial difficulties of reading from computer screens instead of paper, or of note taking on a laptop tablet instead of hand-writing on paper.

But we can use various conditioning techniques to acquire the skills of paperless practices and make them permanent. Here are some general methods for conditioning ourselves to specific behaviors or practices that can be applied for our purpose; some work better than others, depending on the individual.

- Pay attention to and record in your memory the advantages you enjoy each time you complete a paperless practice, then that can function as the favorable stimulus that will reinforce the paperless practice. Another way is to reward yourself with something you enjoy each time you complete a major work task in a paperless manner. According to this conditioning method, which is called positive reinforcement, a behavior is acquired when it is followed by a favorable, or pleasant, stimulus that increases the frequency of the new behavior.

- When you use paperless practices, the increased efficiency will automatically remove certain unpleasant stimuli, such as getting stuck in traffic or searching for a document in a file cabinet. The important thing is to notice the fact that something unlikable is removed from your daily actions when going paperless. According to this conditioning method, which is called negative reinforcement, a certain behavior is acquired when it is followed by the removal of an aversive, or unpleasant, stimulus, which leads to an increase of the behavior's frequency.

- If you fail to go paperless and fall back on paper-based practices, you will soon experience the drawbacks of those. These drawbacks will function as an aversive stimulus when noticed and associated with paper-based practices. This conditioning method is called positive punishment, and according to this a decrease of a certain behavior occurs when that behavior is followed by an aversive, or unpleasant, stimulus.

- Once you stop using paperless practices, the benefits of paperlessness—mobility, decreased clutter, ease of locating documents—would also cease and, when noticed, function as a removed favorable stimulus. This conditioning method is called negative punishment, and according to it when a behavior is followed by the removal of a favorable, or pleasant, stimulus it will result in a decrease of that behavior.

In order for any of these conditioning methods to work, it is essential to be aware of and pay attention to the positive favorable results of doing things in a paperless manner, as well as to the negative and unpleasant results of abandoning paperless work practices.

B. Gradual and incremental adoption

It is very unlikely that anyone who has been using paper-based practices throughout his/her life would manage to switch over to a paperless workstyle overnight, even if s/he had read about and learned all approaches and methods. The most effective and painless approach in becoming paperless is to transition gradually from paper-based to paperless, through incremental changes in practices over time. A sudden attempt to switch over to an all digital way of doing work could bring about a rapid abandonment of the project, resulting from the frustrations of failing and of being unable to complete our tasks.

At different stages during the transition towards a paperless workstyle, there will be many changes in the way we do our work, and adequate time is needed to adapt to, perfect and efficiently adopt a paperless practice. The incremental and gradual transition will allow the use of both digital paperless and paper-based practices in tandem, and this will allow you to temporarily fall back on the paper-based approach if you find a particular paperless practice too difficult to perform, perhaps in a high-pressure situation. It is also a good idea to start implementation of paperless workstyles with less demanding or important tasks until the practice has been fine-tuned and mastered, and feels natural to perform. A realization of the benefits of a paperless workstyle and its overall positive impact on our lives will reinforce the change process and justify the effort.

Of course, it's important not to let the insistence on using digital practices become an obstacle to productivity. If the digital paperless approach becomes too cumbersome, you can revert to paper, but gradually increase the digital approach and become acclimatized to the new paperless way of working.

Finally, it may not be necessary to become 100 percent paperless, but only to change those practices that will be most appropriate and enable greater freedom and time savings. You can still perform certain tasks in a paper-based style if that is most advantageous to, for instance, creativity or flexibility. Hence, different degrees of paperless office digitization can be reached and not everyone needs to become 100 percent paperless. During the course of paperless adoption, you will eventually reach an equilibrium or balance point between digital and paper-based practices that best suits your work tasks and personal workstyle and preferences. Many of the tasks that today may be easier to perform with paper are, however, likely to become more easily implemented in a digital fashion as there is further development of new ICT that can better simulate the specific attributes of paper.

C. Adopting and conditioning of paperless work practices from an organizational perspective

The advantages for organizations in adopting paperless office digitization are numerous, but the switch to paperless will only function if implemented by all or at least a very large fraction of employees in a division or in the entire business. To some degree, we've seen this situation before, when personal computers become available. Colleagues were only able to develop and work on the same documents if they used the same, or at least compatible, software. It was nearly impossible for two collaborators to exchange and work on the same material if one of them was using paperless digitized office practices while the other was paper-based, doing all his/her note-taking and editing in longhand.

A major challenge to a corporation is to introduce paperless office practices in a fashion that ensures rapid adoption rates by the large majority of employees without impairment of performance. A new practice will generally diffuse through an organization at a rate which is dependent on the perceived advantage and gain of the new practice, the risk and the ease of its implementation and use, which, in turn, will depend on its complexity. The return on investment is obviously the main incentive at the corporate leadership level, while the employee may have other motivations for going paperless. All these factors must be taken into account when an adoption strategy is designed and implemented. It's essential that everyone is on board with the change strategy, and that everyone has become convinced of the many benefits they will enjoy. Upper management must recognize that these benefits may differ for employees and employers. This battle will, as usual, start in the mind, and when it has been won there, the rest will merely involve practical and technical implementation.

Implementation is best achieved in a fashion that drives the change process from both ends: top-down and bottom-up. Both ends must first become convinced of the advantages and be motivated to carry out the change in work practices. The most difficult task is to convince employees to become paperless and sustain the change, and in some cases specific incentives that lie in the actual paperlessness itself may have to be provided to sustain motivation and momentum. For example, allowing employees to perform work tasks from out-of-office locations such as home can become a strong incentive once employees realize how much time they save by avoiding the commute.

Essential ingredients for corporate conversion into paperless practices include provision of adequate knowledge about the existence and function of the new paperless practice; persuasion of the value and many advantages of the new practice; and, finally, decisiveness for committing to the adoption of paperless digitized office practices. Ultimately, the process will be completed with a positive confirmation and acceptance that the paperless practices have taken over in a successful manner, thereby reinforcing the gains and advantages.

One effective strategy for adopting paperless practices in an organization is, before adopting it full scale, to initiate it in a pilot scale fashion, where a specific department or section becomes an early adopter. The early adopter will function as a proof or principle for the entire organization, the many advantages being transmitted and highlighted throughout the corporate layers and units. From there, the paperless workstyle will diffuse throughout the organization with less resistance. This type of pilot scale implementation will also aid in resolving technical issues prior to a full scale implementation in which glitches in the system could have broad detrimental impacts.

Finally, the most important factor for succeeding with this change process is the paperless system and practices themselves; ease of use and flawless operation will carry the change process a long way, while a complicated and faulty system will lead to much frustration and resistance.

17. PRACTICAL GUIDE FOR GOING PAPERLESS

It's time to transition to a paperless work- and life style, and in the following sections I will give you concrete practical guidance on how to achieve this.

A. Plan and design your paperless ICT ecosystem

Before buying ICT devices and software, it is essential to thoroughly plan your transition to paperlessness making sure that you purchase the most appropriate types of ICT devices and software for your intended use.

The following example may illustrate this better: Imagine someone who has based his/her paperless system on Windows-PC ICT devices and software, while all his/her clients and collaborators use Apple-based operating systems and ICT devices and software. Despite attempts by these major systems manufacturers to ensure compatibility, there will be, inevitably, an incompatibility that will lead to trouble with file and document sharing and exchange. Other examples of incompatibility are smartphones that are not entirely compatible with mail servers, or scanners that can't scan the appropriate paper formats. Incompatibilities between your ICT system and work practices can have disastrous consequences for your productivity and peace of mind, because you will end up stymied and frustrated.

To achieve a seamlessly integrated use of ICT devices and software—and, therefore, efficient paperless practices without glitches and frustrations—the proper selection of compatible and appropriate ICT is essential.

A rapidly expanding market for a variety of ICT devices and software, or electronic gadgets and programs, has emerged, and new brands, products and models are proliferating and being offered at a rate which is difficult to keep up with, even for the most technology savvy people. Many of these devices are not always perfectly adapted to each other, or sometimes they are completely incompatible, in one or another way. Common incompatibilities are file format and the way devices and software communicate with each other. For instance, some devices communicate through Bluetooth and other through infrared signals. Some devices are compatible with the PC-Windows Office software applications, while others are only compatible with the Apple operating systems software. It is therefore essential to pay attention to such compatibility issues during the design of the integrated ICT system and the selection of devices and software such as mobile wireless devices in relationship to the employer's ICT systems and telecommunications companies. I provide some helpful information on ICT devices and software on my blog at http://enjoypaperless.blogspot.com/.

1. *Map your processes and translate them into paperless with ICT*

One of the initial practical steps in establishing a paperless ICT system is to figure out which processes you are currently using for work task completion, and how these can be converted into paperless. This is also an opportunity to make certain changes in the actual process flow and organization of your work, and to optimize it.

One generic approach that can be used to initiate the transition to a paperless process gradually and smoothly is the following set of steps:

1. Make a list of your current paper-based practices and rank them in order according their importance and frequency of use.
2. Determine the degree of interconnectivity of each task with the other tasks. If, for example , you organize your documents in different folders and drawers, then which of these will be placed in the same drawer and which in the same folder.
3. Determine if there are certain types of documents used as a basis to generate other types of document, and if there are some types of documents dependent on others.
4. Determine the intensity of collaboration for each task and estimate how much each task will be worked on by or with collaborators.
5. Based on the above information, draw a map of each current paper-based process, and then translate it into a paperless process by drawing the integrated paperless process plan for each task. For example, the paperless process map for manuscript editing may look like this: **a.** receiving the manuscript per snail-mail from the client **b.** scanning the manuscript into electronic format; **c.** convert scanned image to text file; **d.** saving the scanned manuscript in the client's folder; **e.** editing the manuscript using a specific word processing software; **f.** if the work is done on several computers, then use specific

software and media to transfer the file between them; **g.** email the edited manuscript to the client and wait for response on your comments; **h.** interact with the client per Internet-based messenger to discuss specific editing issues of the manuscript; **i.** make notes of this communication per hand-writing on a tablet-PC; **j.** store the note file in the client subfolder; **k.** make some final editing to the manuscript; **l.** create an electronic invoice using a template form and save it to the client's folder; **m.** email the edited manuscript along with the invoice to the client; **n.** check your Internet-based payment account for the money transfer.

6. Next integrate the individual paperless process maps, for the different work tasks, into one map where common processes are highlighted– and linked through common ITC components and tasks.

This map will help you to define the various ICT processes, devices and software that you will need. It may be best to start this paperless conversion by picking one simple and easy to implement process, because early success is important for gaining momentum to complete the whole system. Once this first process has been converted into paperless you can expand from this into other processes and projects.

Another good way to decide which ICT devices and software to acquire for converting your paper-based processes is the following: Make a table with all your individual work tasks, each placed in one row (for example: email communication, messenger communication, scanning paper documents, scanning pictures, editing texts documents, writing text documents, taking hand-written notes, taking audio notes, etc.) and then think of all the ICT devices and software that you could use for these tasks and place each of them in one column (e.g., PDA, PDA-phone, tablet-PC, laptop, desktop, flatbed scanner, word processing software X, word processing software Y, and so on). Then you'll link each task will all devices that can perform that task in the table. This should eventually lead to a spreadsheet that enables you to see which devices and software will be the most appropriate for selection, i.e., those that can perform the most tasks.

Once you have selected the types of ICT devices and software your paperless system will consist of, you'll need to decide on which specific brands and models to acquire for your paperless system. For this you'll need to consider their compatibility between them, your collaborators' paperless systems, and the required degree of mobility of your paperless system and the budget that you can allocate to acquire it.

2. *Ensure compatibility between ICT components*

The compatibility or "ecology" of ITC components and software is one of the most important considerations. A variety of devices and software exist, and not all of them are compatible in terms of operating systems, file format and wireless networking. It's essential to make sure that the various components of the integrated paperless process are fully compatible. New models appear on the market continuously and offer a variety of functionalities. This may create confusion and doubt as to what to buy. In fact, you will in most cases face the dilemma of having to choose from among dozens of different ICT devices that all have more or less the same specifications. In these cases, you will have to consider parameters such as cost, aesthetics, preferred brands and customer reviews. It may also be useful to keep in mind that devices of the same brand (i.e. laptop, printer and digital camera) are more likely to be compatible with each other to a greater extent than devices of different brands. This becomes important for achieving a seamless integration. Also, pay attention to the upgradeability of devices, particularly for computers; the potential to upgrade hard drives and memory can prolong the useable life span of a computer by several years.

Many ICT devices' functional attributes are unnecessary and sometimes even useless. For example, some smartphones have built-in cameras with an impressive (or excessive) resolution, while their small size and low-quality lenses will not allow for high quality pictures—regardless of resolution. Another example is laptops with built-in webcams, which are useless for those who have no intention of using them for video communications. Certain attributes, such as memory, hard drive storage size and computing speed/power are in most cases worth investing in, because these things will allow you to use the ICT device for a longer period before having to buy new. It is also worth spending a bit more for quality, instead of cutting corners and ending up with devices that won't have all the necessary functional attributes, are dysfunctional, have a short lifespan or will need repairs frequently. This kind of frugality becomes much more costly in the long run, considering the negative impact, on you and your work practices.

Having devices with multiple capabilities can offer great advantages if that translates into not having to carry multiple devices. For instance, a smartphone with built-in camera, Internet capability, mp3 player and even a GPS can reduce the number of independent devices from four to one. While the quality of these attributes (i.e. photography, GPS map tracking, music playing) may be somewhat inferior in these multi-integrated devices to those in specialized individual devices, the positive trade-offs of having to carry and charge less will, in most cases, out-weigh these quality compromises.

Another aspect to pay attention to is to avoid redundancies in device functionalities. For example, traveling with a laptop, smartphone and digital camera, all with photography capabilities, means that you are traveling with three cameras. Whatever you do, avoid shopping for ICT devices and software on impulse, but always spend time researching them in advance, comparing different brands and models, and even vendors.

3. *Ensure compatibility with the work environment*

The type of ICT that our work environment, collaborators and clients use is important to consider when deciding on what types and brands of ICT devices and software to acquire. It can be very frustrating to have to convert file formats each time you exchange a text with a collaborator, or to be unable to connect to printers and other peripheral devices at the work place only because the computer does not support those systems, or to be unable to use software that the employer provides for free because of operating system incompatibilities. Specific things to ensure compatibility for are: hardware (i.e., compatibility between printers and computers), software (i.e., compatibility between operating systems and software), and modes of communication (i.e., compatibility between messenger software and remote access software).

4. *Consider your required degree of mobility*

Your mobility requirement is important to consider. If you intend to do most of your work from home, then a desktop system will work fine, but if you need to travel often, while working, then you'll need an ICT device and software that is compatible with a high level of mobility—perhaps a laptop, a PDA-phone, and software that enables you to access your employer's database easily. In general, if we need a high degree of mobility, then smaller and lighter portable ICT devices that can connect to multiple types of networks are better. Specific mobility factors to consider for the choice of ICT are whether you have long or short commutes, travel by automobile or train, and whether you travel long distances and stay away from the home base for extended periods. Commuting by automobile will not enable you to type or read, so you would need an ICT device that has audio capabilities, enabling you to speak your notes or listen to a text instead of reading it. If you expect to travel for extended periods of time, then you may want to consider a fairly powerful laptop that has capacities comparable to a desktop. Portable scanners, printers and keyboards are also devices to consider for those who need more sophisticated office capabilities while on the move.

5. *Calibrate according to your budget*

You need to determine the available budget for your paperless ICT system: We cannot plan on using a very expensive ICT system, which might consist of multiple large high-definition monitors and a high-end computer, when we don't have the adequate budget for that. The budget will also depend on the required quality and capacity, in terms of durability and computing power—and these parameters are, in turn, dependent on the type of work practices and intensity of use. It will often pay off, in the long term, to invest in a better quality system, instead of having to upgrade or repair every once in a while, or even become compromised.

One of the first things to do is to determine the available budget for acquiring the paperless ICT system. A cost/benefit analysis can be useful to perform, where the gains related to increased productivity, lesser need to travel, lesser need to maintain office space and a potentially better quality of life is weighed against the cost of acquiring the paperless ICT system and the time invested in learning how to use it. Make an estimate of how much money you will save by going paperless based on these parameters, but keep in mind that not everything can be measured in terms of money. Certain quality of life attributes, such as spending more time with family, is not necessarily a monetary gain. For such cases, you will have to determine how much value they have in monetary terms (this is what, in economics lingo, is called the opportunity cost) and factor that into your estimation of what you are willing to pay for your paperless ICT system.

B. Acquire and set up your paperless ICT system

Once you have established the specific types of tasks, work fashion, intensity and mode of travel, communication needs and the ICT system specifications of those collaborators and employees with whom you need to maintain compatibility, it is time to select and acquire devices. The selection of ICT components has a lot in common with shopping. When you shop you are likely to change your mind about which components to purchase.

The Internet is a good resource for conducting research and obtaining and comparing specifications, costs and independent customer reviews for different ICT devices and software. The number of devices and systems that you normally would have needed several days and visits to several different shops to see, can be viewed on the Internet in a couple of hours, or even less than that. One potential drawback to Internet shopping, , though, is that it is more difficult to investigate the compatibility between different devices, compared to visiting a store and obtaining direct face-to-face guidance on such matters. Nor will the Internet allow you to see and operate the actual device. A solution to this may be to identify suitable ICT devices and software through the Internet, and then visit the stores and specifically look at those items before purchasing them. Almost all software is available through the Internet today, in a convenient and instantly downloadable manner. You will in most cases also have the opportunity to test a demo of a software prior to deciding on whether you want to purchase it or not. In fact, shopping for your ICT-based paperless system online is a major paperless endeavor. I provide some information on specific systems and application on my blog at http://enjoypaperless.blogspot.com/.

Once you have acquired all your components, it is time to set them up; connect them, install them, and make sure they are optimally functional in a seamlessly integrated way. This may take some time, depending on the number of devices and the complexity of applications. And the process of optimizing the system may even take several weeks, as you discover ways to make the system more functional through use, and as you fine tune different attributes while working with it. When you buy the ICT components, make sure to always keep the original boxes at least until you feel confident that the device is for you, in case you decide to return it. Always read the instruction manuals before operating the device, because this can save you time and prevent your destroying the device. Use the device manufacturer's and service provider's help lines (either through the Internet or telephone) to get assistance with how to install and set up the various devices and software in an integrated manner.

An example of a paperless ICT system for the frequent traveler

A frequent traveler must consider the following factors for establishing a convenient and productive ICT system: weight, portability, international compatibility, power supply, Internet connection capabilities and ruggedness. The most important features to focus on may be weigh and portability. A small and lightweight laptop with adequate computing power and low power consumption, integrated webcam and wireless Wi-Fi and Bluetooth capabilities would work well for lightweight versatile computing on the go. If you plan on getting work done while traveling by air or need to make notes by hand you should then consider a tablet-laptop since it is more convenient to work on in the cramped space of an airplane seat and can be used for handwriting. An unlocked quad-band (capable of wireless telephony in all regions of our world) PDA-phone with Bluetooth capability would serve as a complementary ICT device to the laptop. This device will provide you with email communication and access to the Internet at location where Wi-Fi is unavailable. The PDA-pone will also give you multimedia capabilities such as watching movies or listening to music. An unlocked phone will enable you to use cheap local pay-as-you-go sim cards instead of paying for the expensive roaming services if you intend to make frequent use of telephone communications. Alternatively, you can buy or rent a simple cell phone for the duration of your stay abroad. The Bluetooth headset would enable hands-free telephone communication through the PDA-phone and chatting through the laptop computer when connected to the Internet. An extra battery for the laptop will be useful for long distance flights or other occasions when electricity grid access is unavailable. If you like reading books while traveling then an eBook reader is a must, alternatively you can load eBooks on, and read them from, the laptop or PDA-phone, but remember that these latter alternatives are power consuming and won't allow for many hours of reading without recharging. A flash memory drive, or a portable hard drive, is good to have for safe backup and storage of important documents. An ethernet cable could become handy if you would have access to a LAN socket. Make sure to bring appropriate power plug convertors if you travel internationally.

Useful software for the mobile worker are convertors for currency and other measurements, foreign language dictionaries and language training software.

Useful services that one can subscribe to are international telephone roaming and wireless, or Wi-Fi, Internet access point software that allows you to access the Internet at thousands of airports, hotels and café's worldwide at a charge that is directly deducted from your credit card. Another useful service is one that enables access to your office or home main computer in case you would not have all your documents with you on the laptop. These software allow you to operate your remote computer as if you where at home or in your office. An Internet-based data archiving and backup service can be handy to upload documents safely and protect them from loss in case your luggage would get stolen together with your portable hard drive and memory stick. You can alternatively email important documents to yourself and thereby store them safely on mail servers. Some cellphone service providers offer pay-as-you-go Internet access modems that connect to your computer and provide wireless Internet access through the cellular phone system. Another, but slow, approach to connect wirelessly to the internet is to access a dial-up service by connecting the laptop to the cell phone through Bluetooth.

There are certainly many variations of suitable ICT systems for the frequent traveler -mobile worker- and doing a thorough homework for selecting a well-adapted system for your specific needs will always pay back.

Look at http://enjoypaperless.blogspot.com for real life examples of paperless ICT systems and uses for travelers.

C. Specific work tasks: transition from paper-based to paperless

Digitization requires consideration of the type of work practices we perform. Some of the most common categories of work practices and the ICT components required for those are:

1. *Document generation and editing*

ICT has already had an enormous impact on the way we generate and edit documents today. It is rare to hand-write longer texts, while typing into a laptop or desktop computer is the most common way of generating and editing text documents. Creating digital documents from paper-based documents is also an essential step in the process of switching over to a paperless workstyle. We will look at different ways to create digital documents in a paperless fashion, or at least end up with a paperless format.

- Hand-written texts:

If your work involves the creation or editing of hand-written documents, then you'll need ICT devices geared toward that task. Hand-written documents contain more information than just the actual text, embedded into the actual writing style. Character, personality traits and the psychological state of an individual can be inferred through his/her or her hand writing style. This information would become lost if it was translated into typed text. Hand-writing gives the documents a more personal feel, which may be advantageous and desired for certain situations and work tasks. In general, devices that have digital hand-writing capabilities have a touch screen that can sense the point of the pen, or even your finger, and translate the movement into an image in a way that mimics a pen on a paper. Other devices are actual pens that write on paper but the movement on the paper is recorded digitally and translated into a digital image. Devices and methods with hand-writing capabilities are:

A PDA (personal digital assistant) *or PDA-phone* can be used to scribble down notes and is ideal if you need a high level of mobility and the option of starting the device rapidly. The drawback is the small screen area, which makes it complicated to generate comprehensive texts, but can to some extent be addressed by linking an external portable keyboard to the PDA.

A tablet computer is ideal if you want to enjoy note-taking capabilities similar to a regular size note book and have a letter size viewable page to use. The tablets are also easier to write on, because of the size and because the higher processing power allows for a variety of writing qualities (color, pen size and pressure). Another advantage of the tablet is the availability of any other applications that can be run by the processor (similar to a regular laptop) such as word processing programs, Internet and email. Some tablets consist simply of a one-piece screen and all text and data entry has to be done through that screen with a pen. Other tablet computers also have a keyboard with a pointing device, identical to those found on laptops. The screen can basically be turned around and folded over the keyboard, providing tablet capabilities. The latter device has the additional advantage of being a regular laptop with a keyboard, while the former is lighter. The drawback of a tablet here is the relatively large size and weight, as well as power consumption, which may limit you to a few hours between each battery charge, unless you have access to a power source.

A note pad is a pad that can be connected to the computer and used to write on with a pen, and this hand-written text will then be transferred to the computer (desktop or laptop). A note pad is a peripheral device that lacks the mobility of the PDA and tablet, because it needs to be linked to a computer, but it may represent the optimal way of integrating hand-written note-taking and drawing capabilities to a desktop computer system.

A digital pen is a somewhat bulky pen with a small integrated camera that records the movement of the pen on a specific type of paper, and stores that information in its internal memory. It can later be connected to a computer and the data transferred into a software that can display the hand-written notes. This method does not substitute for paper entirely, because you still end up writing on paper, but storage and reading of the document is finally done in a paperless digital format.

Digitizing hand-written paper documents as images. Under certain circumstances paper may simply be the most convenient or even only possible medium for generating documents, in conjunction with hand-writing. One can, however, digitize these documents by scanning the hand-written document into electronic format and saving it as an image. This is a convenient way of generating documents and also allows for inserting drawings into the document directly. This method is, however, only partially paperless, as it requires the use of paper, but the archiving and dissemination of the text is finally done electronically.

- Typed texts:

If your texts need to be in a typed format, or you simply prefer to type instead of hand-writing, then you need a device with a keyboard, or capability to convert hand-written or spoken text into a typed text format.

Typing in the text through a keyboard is the most common way of entering text and generating documents and is usually performed through a QWERTY-type keyboard. A variety of alternative keyboards, which don't depend on the QWERTY model, have been developed to enable more efficient, ergonomic and easier text entry. Some of these can be operated with one hand in a mobile fashion. Regardless of the type of keyboard, efficient document generation through typing requires the acquisition of "touch typing," or "blind typing" skills, which can produce up to 90 words per minute when handled skillfully. There are on the market a variety of training software for learning blind typing, and they can enable the user to learn typing on a time-independent and cost-effective schedule. If you need a small form factor and high degree of mobility, then a PDA-phone or other type of ultra-light portable computer will work. Even a smartphone with a numeric key pad can work, but text generation may not be as efficient as when using a full size QWERTY keyboard.

Hand-writing and subsequent digitization. Typing in text through a keyboard can sometimes be complicated because of space constraints, such as in an airplane or on the go. Some people never seem to be able to get the typing right and are therefore much slower and make many mistakes when entering text through a keyboard. For those cases, it is possible to hand-write the text into the documents through a tablet-PC or through a write pad connected to the PC in conjunction with specific software that saves it into a document as hand-written text or translates it into typed text. The hand-written text can be entered through a text recognition interface (software) that translates it into typed text—but to enable accurate translation into typed text by the OCR software, you will need to polish your hand-writing style. The tablet-PC and write pad were described in the previous section on hand-written text generation. An alternative approach is to write the original text per hand on a paper, then scan the paper and translate the hand-written text to typed text with the same type of software that was described above.

Generation of typed text through speech recognition. Another method for generating typed text is the use of speech recognition software that recognizes the spoken words and translates them into text. This approach is extremely powerful in that it can allow text entry at conditions that make typing or hand-writing impossible, such as when driving a car. The speech can be either directly entered through a microphone connected to the computer, or indirectly through a portable digital recording device from which the text is subsequently transferred to the computer. There is a variety of speech recognition software, which initially needs to be trained for the users' specific pronunciation and can then interface with a variety of software and applications to enable speech recognition mediated text and command entry. The major obstacle with this means of electronic text generation is the need for speech clarity and consistency. The way we pronounce words and sentences can greatly vary and depend on our mood or physical state, and thereby complicate the translation into electronic text, resulting in numerous errors. However, the development of speech recognition software continues to advance and will render this mode of document generation feasible for most users in the near future.

Editing texts. For text editing the same approach for writing texts applies, while a tablet may work very well here because of the lesser need to type large texts. Editing mostly involves corrections and changes of only some of the text. The hand-writing capability of a tablet-PC will also enable editing and annotating of the texts in a fashion similar to paper-based systems, where hand-written notes are made directly into the typed text.

Converting existing paper documents to digital. One of the first things you must do before implementing a paperless work system is to decide on what to do with your existing paper documents, and the paper documents that you may henceforth receive from clients and collaborators. The important thing to keep in mind is to make sure that there is no loss of documents and information—therefore, archiving, management and recovery of electronic and the potential paper-based documents must be part of a well-planned paperless office system. In many cases, regulations or even the law will dictate whether certain paper documents can be scanned and destroyed, or not, even if scanned into a digital format. It is essential to know the relevant rules in those cases.

The fact that a very large proportion of text is still only available to us through paper-based media such as books, and the fact that not everyone we exchange documents with will decide on going paperless, means that we will inevitably have to digitize large numbers of paper-based documents. Fortunately, this can today be done with relative ease. A variety of paper document scanners exist on the market, specialized for specific types of applications, such as book scanning, receipt and business card scanning. There are also portable scanners that can enable document scanning while traveling. Paper document scanners with automatic paper feeders (similar to those found on copy machines) provide a convenient automatic way of digitizing large text documents that can be separated into individual papers. These scanners can scan both sides of papers and automatically translate the text to editable text through OCR, and save them as, for instance, PDF or Microsoft Word files. There are also pen-size scanners that are handheld and battery-operated. They scan in word by word and are operated like a highlighting pen (slide 12 in appendix).

Scanners often come with free OCR software, but it may make sense to separately purchase the best OCR software available. OCR software takes an image from the scanner, and puts searchable letters and words in the file based on the words it can recognize in the image. For example, let's say you have a page that has some pictures and text. The OCR software should pick out most of the text and include that text as "invisibly" searchable in the file. The best OCR software recognizes more than 90 percent of the "typed" text correctly. If you are disappointed that the software only picks up 90 percent of the words, remember that zero percent of your paper filing system is computer searchable. Don't expect OCR software to recognize hand printed characters easily.

*Converting books into digital media.*_While digital paperless books have become quite popular in the past years, many books are still only available in paper format, and the only way of converting them into a paperless format is by scanning. Automatic book scanners exist, and they are designed to turn pages automatically and capture images of each page through digital cameras. These devices are costly and usually operated by book scanning service companies. There are cheaper book scanners on the market, but they have to be operated manually. They're not suited for large-scale, high-throughput book scanning, but they do provide an interesting way for students to save money on books given that the copyright regulations are respected, or the executive who loves having his/her library available to her/him while on the go.

Paper scanning services. One can outsource the paper document and book scanning to companies that provide such services. This is most likely the most effective approach for corporate users who need to scan large amounts of documents. These companies also offer other associated services, such as archiving, organizing, and paper shredding.

- Audio and Video media:

Audio notes. Audio note-taking is very effective when you need to take notes on the go, or when your hands are used for something else, or when you can't carry anything larger than a pen, or when you need to interview someone and there is no time or space for taking hand-written notes. You can use a digital dictaphone to take audio notes, and there are a variety of such devices on the market. They are usually small enough to fit in a pocket and can operate on batteries for hours. These devices usually have a file or directory system so that notes can be organized in different categories and also transferred to a computer, and stored or shared with other people. Audio notes can also be converted to typed text using speech recognition software that translates the notes to typed text after transferring them to the computer. An alternative and more traditional way_is to listen to the notes and manually type them into digital format.

Video notes. Another less common method for taking notes is to record them as videos. You can use a PDA-phone, a cell phone, a webcam connected to a computer or a video camera, and basically point it yourself while you're talking. A video note is more personalized, because it conveys information beyond the actual spoken words, via facial expressions and body language, and gestures that are visible through these media. For these reasons, video notes or messages can be very powerful substitutes for face-to-face interactions.

- What works best for me?

It would be impossible to address all possible combinations of situations and parameters that would set a rule for which method of text generations is the most suitable for each one of these. However, there are some general guidelines that may help you in figuring out the most efficient and appropriate method. The method of choice, and consequently also the ICT devices and software for generating texts, will mainly depend on the type of text (e.g., larger comprehensive texts or shorter notes) that is to be generated, the conditions (e.g., is a regular office available, or do we mostly work from an airplane seat) and what personal preferences we have (e.g., for some people it is easier to hand-write than type and vice versa). Some of the following examples may help get you started on deciding which ICT is the best for you for text generation.

- Someone who is good at tying on a keyboard, but spends a lot of time traveling by plane should consider getting a tablet laptop computer, which would allow her/him to type in text at common office conditions or whenever s/he has enough space to place the laptop on his/her lap, while when s/he travels on the plane s/he can still read text and enter text through hand writing.
- Someone who has great difficulties with typing should consider a system that allows for hand-writing and subsequent conversion of the hand-written text to typed text. S/He should also consider a voice recognition software with the appropriate microphone for text generation.

- Someone who only needs to take shorter notes can consider using a small and handy PDA rather than the larger and heavier laptop.
- Someone who requires typing capability but has very limited space and a need to be mobile most of the time should consider an ultra light smaller version laptop that can fit in a larger coat pocket.

You would of course also have to consider the reading and communications requirements together with the text generation and editing requirements when selecting the most appropriate device.

- Transition from paper-based writing:

Generating texts is most likely something that most people have been doing through keyboards anyway; it is less likely that someone would write larger comprehensive texts by hand these days—but some of us still do. The transition to a paperless way of writing has to occur gradually. It will be immensely useful to learn touch, or blind, typing if you need to generate larger texts. Hand-writing on a PDA or tablet-PC requires some training, especially when that text is to be translated into typed text. Using speech recognition software will also require training the software with regard to how you pronounce words, and then maintaining consistency in the way you pronounce. All these means for text generation and editing are already used by millions of people and there is no reason why you should not be able to figure out the best way of doing it for your specific purpose and conditions.

2. *Reading documents*

There are a variety of ways to "read" electronic documents, and these can be categorized in the following main groups: visually reading typed text, listening to typed text through a text-to-speech translator, or listening to audio recorded text. Some other specialized methods also exist, such as touch-based reading for the visually impaired.

Reading from a monitor. Direct reading from the screen of a laptop, tablet-PC, or desktop monitor is currently the most common way of reading electronic documents and this is most frequently done through word processing and document reader software or a web browser. Advantages of word processors and some document reader software include the capacity to edit, mark and comment on the actual texts. In fact, most reading from a computer screen is done while editing or writing documents. Continuous improvements in monitor technology, and the development of lighter and more energy efficient laptop computers in combination with better batteries, render this way of document reading more feasible for longer periods without suffering from eye strain. Reading from computer monitors is, in most cases, done in combination with editing or making comments on the text, or copying parts of the text. This process will also be greatly improved with large displays or multiple monitors. In this way, you won't have to deal with multiple overlapping windows for the different applications or documents that you work on.

Reading from smaller screens. Smartphones, PDAs and portable media players have also become common interfaces for document reading, and there is specialized software for those devices that can enable the reading of the most common text document formats. These may be particularly useful devices for reading during short commutes on trains or buses. You can also use personal video glasses to read computer-based texts from a word processor, document reader or web browser. These types of glasses were mainly developed for watching movies and the recent improvement in resolution now allows high-definition display. They can be connected to a portable media player or laptop computer that supports the desired document format. The main advantage of these devices for document reading is that they allow for hands-free reading in a dark environment such as during a flight.

Electronic paper- eBook readers. A new type of document reading devices appearing on the market are based on electronic ink, and they can display text and pictures in gray scale. Their screens have a paper-like appearance with a dark gray text against a light gray or white background. The screen is, similar to a paper, not back-lit, so a light source is necessary for reading. The main advantage of such devices is the portability—they can be made as compact as a thin paperback book and very lightweight. The most striking advantage is their low energy consumption; these devices only consume electricity when the page is changed, and can therefore be used for reading tens of books with one single battery charge. With a memory card one can easily have hundreds of books and documents stored and accessible at any time (slide 15 in appendix). The electronic ink technology is rapidly evolving and several electronics manufacturers and Internet-based bookstores have already launched different models on the market. Some of these devices also have an integrated mp3 music player allowing for simultaneous music listening while reading. Some of these allow purchasing and downloading of books wirelessly from eBook stores. These devices will soon have backlit color screens, marking capabilities, extended memory, Internet connection capabilities and also be bendable as paper. When these devices will be equipped with speech reading capability, they will provide the ultimate document and book reading experience and flexibility. Users can already have thousands of books readily available at their fingertips while on the go with these devices.

Speech reading. Another way of reading typed text is through the use of text-to-speech translation software that can convert text into audible speech. Such software is currently undergoing major developments that enable for better pronunciation and a more human-like voice. This application is particularly useful when we need to be focused on something else and cannot hold a device or focus our sight on a text, when driving, for example. Electronic ink devices capable of text-to-speech translation and audio-book reading will in the future provide the ultimate mobile book reading capability.

Audio book reading. Audio books have existed since the emergence of the first tape recorders, while their versatility and usage have proliferated dramatically in recent years through the extended storage capacity of mp3 files in combination with larger memory capacity. Several Internet-based book stores market all sort of books as audio files that can be listened to through a computer, mp3 player, PDA and even mobile phones. Audio books come in one of two formats: (1) the unabridged format that contains the entire original book, or (2) the abridged format, which is an abbreviated version of the original typed book. The greatest advantage of audio books is that they can be listened to while performing other, intellectually non-demanding tasks such as driving, jogging, or even performing repetitive work. A common problem with this type of media has to do with license and copy protection, and often leads to some limitations with regard to the compatibility with mobile media players.

But the use of audio books is a great way of converting otherwise dead time to more productive, educational or entertaining time. One can, for example, through a portable media player connected to a wireless headset, very flexibly learn about specific subjects while commuting to work, even if the commute involves transitions between different means of transportation. When increased attention to the outer world is required, you can simply pause the book reading and then restart it after boarding the next train.

Audio-video media viewing. A variety of education and entertainment media exist as video or audio, and in these formats they can provide an unprecedented learning experience. In the past, such media could only be experienced through stationary TVs, desktop computers or laptops. The recent development of video-capable portable multimedia devices and wearable high-definition LCD monitors (video glasses) allow us to enjoy this material on the go in a very flexible and portable manner.

- What works best for me?

As with text generation, the most optimal way of reading texts will depend on the type of texts, conditions and personal preferences. While most people who regularly use computers have read texts from a monitor, they may be less inclined to do so for larger texts and longer times. This is where the many years of conditioning to paper has made us so used to that medium, to the point that it feels awkward to start reading entire documents or books from a monitor. The electronic paper (or electronic ink)-based devices are more paper-like in their appearance and may therefore be more suitable for book and magazine reading. A tablet computer is ideal for this since it can be held like a paper-based notebook.

- Transition from paper-based reading:

The way to transition to a paperless way of reading is, again, gradual and incremental adaption. Don't try to switch over to a hundred percent paperless reading in one go, but start with reading only some documents entirely from the screen. Remind yourself of the tradeoffs when it gets hard to read text in a digital manner. With time, you will notice that it becomes more natural and easier to read from a monitor, and finally at some point you will even consider it better than reading from a paper.

Display technology is evolving rapidly and the market will soon offer devices with a close to hundred percent paper-like reading experience.

3. Communications

A key advantage of going paperless is the fact that you can very easily communicate electronic documents and media through a variety of means. Some work tasks require continuous interaction with multiple partners, and this will pose particular challenges for the selection of appropriate ICT devices, software and communication services. Here we need to determine the type and intensity of communications capability that we require, and whether we need capacity to communicate from multiple locations in a flexible manner, or simply only from our home residence. There are two main types of communications channels: the Internet and telephony. In the past, these were more distinct, while in recent years the borders between them have become somewhat blurred, as we can use the Internet for telephony, and the cellular phone networks can be used to send text messages similar to email. Further blurring the distinction, Internet can be accessed through a telephony connection with the use of a modem. Telephony networks are, however, mostly used for live audio or speech communications, while the Internet can be used for live and for static non-direct communications such as email. The low cost of Internet has made it into a primarily live communication channel, and in particular, for long distance communications, while mobile, or cellular, telephony is mostly used for mobile communications while on the go. Cellular networks with high speed and high capacity data transfer have however already enabled Internet-based mobile telephony.

i.Connection to the telephony networks. There are three main modes of connection to telephone networks: (1) the land line, (2) a cellular network, or, (3) a wireless satellite network. While the landline may allow for faster data transfer rates, which is good for fax transmission and Internet, its main disadvantage is that it lacks mobility outside of the periphery of your house. One can use a wireless phone system connected to the landline, but that usually only provides a few hundred yards of connection range. The cellular networks have become popular and provide the advantage of mobility. The newer generations of cellular networks can also allow for fast data transfer rates that can enable even video transmission. Most cellular telephony companies provide international roaming capabilities, which means that you can access the telephony network through another cellular company when you are outside of your provider's network range. However, not all areas are covered by cell phone networks, and in the case of traveling to such a place, and still requiring telephony services, you would need a satellite phone. These devices can connect to the telephony network directly through satellite. These systems and associated services are quite expensive and the devices are significantly bulkier than the regular cell phones. Cellular phones are slowly taking over the landline-based telephony, and are continuously evolving and enabling faster connections and the devices are becoming increasingly comprehensive, such as the PDA-phones and smartphones that enable Internet and email access through the cellular network.

ii.Connection to the Internet. There are a variety of ways to connect to the Internet:

- Telephone landline-based dial-up services by which a desktop or laptop computer, with a dial-up modem, is connected to the telephone jack. The main advantages of this type of connection are the low price and the option to connect to the Internet from wherever a landline connection is available. The main disadvantage is the very slow connection speed compared to most other means of Internet connection.

- Another telephone landline-based Internet connection is the DSL (digital subscriber line) through which a desktop or laptop computer with a modem can connect. An external modem is connected to the DSL through the telephone jack and provides the access to the Internet directly to the computer through a cable or via a wireless router or Wi-Fi. The Wi-Fi allows access to the DSL connection wirelessly within a certain periphery, which usually covers the residence. The main advantages of DSL connections are the fast connection speeds and low cost, while a major disadvantage is the lack of mobility; you can't take the DSL connection with you or access it from any landline other than the subscribed residence.

- One can access the Internet at comparable capacities to the DSL connection through a cable TV line. This type of connection will also require a modem and the advantages and disadvantages are more or less the same as telephone line-based DSL connections.

- Satellite-based connections exist and are independent on telephone landlines and can therefore be used at locations that are not supported by such. These systems are however expensive and may therefore only make sense to deploy when they can serve many users.

- Wireless broadband can allow connection wirelessly from any location supported by the network. These networks are commonly accessed by laptops and smartphones by mobile workers while on the go.

- Mobile phone network-based Internet connections exist, and their speed is dependent on the cellular network type. These are almost exclusively used for accessing Internet from PDA-phones and smartphones.

Once we have settled on a way to communicate through Internet or telephony networks, we can start interacting with others through ICT. These communications can take any of the following formats.

- Live / real-time communications:

Audio-Video. This is the closest we can get to simulate a live face-to-face communication, and it involves both visual and audio interaction. This type of communication is today most commonly done through Internet with a webcam connected to a computer. A variety of free software and services are available through the Internet for this type of communication. Another, more sophisticated, Internet-based version is done with specialized teleconferencing equipment and software. This will usually enable a video transfer of a higher resolution and thereby render the communication more life-like. The cellular telephony networks are in some countries so advanced that they enable live video communication with mobile phones. These devices have a video camera on the same side as the monitor/screen that is pointed towards the speaker during the communication. As I mentioned earlier, video communication in which each of the communication partners can see the other is more personal and conveys more information than voice communication alone. This is also why face-to-face communication is so important; a large proportion of communications taking place between two or more individuals is conveyed by nonverbal means which are difficult to transmit through ICT. One way to overcome this obstacle, at least to some degree, is to use a high resolution webcam with a high quality audio system and thereby enhance the audiovisual details of the communication that will make it more life-like. Another way to optimize communications through a webcam system is to make sure that at least the upper part of our body, from the waist and up, is visible in the field of sight. This will enable much of the communication that is conveyed through the body language and gesticulations to get through.

A fast connection is required for this type of communication to enable the transfer of the video signal. This mode of communication is also a good way to make sure that the person you communicate with is the one you think it is.

Voice. This is the most common type of communication today, and it's mainly done through landline and cell phones. But Internet-based voice communication and even telephony is rapidly gaining ground against the traditional telephony, mainly because of more competitive prices. In fact, voice and video communication can be achieved at no cost through the Internet, if a connection is available. We can also use Internet-based communication channels to interact with cell and land line phones. This is particularly cost-effective for long-distance communications.

Text. Live text messaging is a common way to chat through the Internet. This way of communication is often done in situations where anonymity is desired; the communicating partners must rely on the information they receive from the person they interact with to know who it is. This type of communication is often done in a semi-live manner, in that we can type a message, send it to our partner, and, once s/he sees it, s/he will reply, and so forth. Internet text communication is most commonly done through a common QWERTY keyboard, but can also be done through a speech recognition software in which one speaks the messages, or less commonly through hand-writing on a tablet computer or write pad. Text communication is also commonly done through the cellular telephony network and phones as text messages. This type of communication is also semi-live for the same reasons outlined above, and the messages are also short due to the limits of text generation on a numeric key pad and the small screen of mobile phones that makes it difficult to compose longer and more comprehensive texts. This type of message communication is frequently also charged to the cell phone subscriber.

- Static communication:

This takes place in a non-live manner and is similar, but much faster, to old-fashioned snail mail communication in which letters are exchanged between the communicating partners. Email is the most common type of communication and is done through the Internet. One can use the email platform to send written text messages, audio messages or video messages in the form of short movies, and the same attributes of these methods apply here for those outlined for live communications. In fact, many types of communications are semi-live, because they may occur in real time but still involve rapid responses. If an Internet or telephony network is unavailable, you can still communicate though ICT in a static manner by exchanging the messages on a physical storage media through snail mail.

- Communications between ICT components:

Many of your ICT devices need to communicate between them to enable work tasks. For example, the main computer has to be capable of communications with scanners, printers and other peripherals. It is therefore essential to ensure communication compatibility between different ICT devices when we are setting up our paperless system. Using peripherals that interact with the computer through the same type of connection is likely to minimize the probability of a connection incompatibility since most computers are not equipped with all types of connection technologies. The purchasing peripherals and a computer of the same brand will also in most cases ensure connection compatibility. There are four main wire-based communication systems used to connect peripherals to the main computer: USB, firewire, serial port and parallel port. The two latter are becoming less common while the USB is the most common and the firewire connection enables faster data transfer speeds. The main wireless ICT device communication types are the Wi-Fi, Bluetooth and infrared. While all computers and many peripherals are equipped with at least one wire –based communication type, it is a good idea to make sure that it also has a wireless connection technology.

- What works best for me?

This will depend on several factors such as your required intensity and frequency of communication, the available communication systems at your working locations or the places that you travel to, and also your personal preferences. A PDA-phone is almost a must for the busy professional who needs integrated phone, email, calendar and some Internet capabilities on the go. For this you'll need a cellular phone service provider that can support these capabilities. Before choosing one, look at their national and international geographic coverage maps to make sure you can use the device when traveling. For your home connection, you may want to make a choice based on available services, connection speed and capacity and cost. Most households have either a telephone line-based DSL or a cable TV line-based Internet connection, and these are usually quite comparable. If you live in cities with Wi-Fi wireless Internet service providers, you may want to investigate this option, because it will give allow you to access Internet at your residence but also at any other location in the city. The wireless broadband services are an interesting option for the frequent traveler who needs Internet access in multiple cities nationwide. For the low-intensity user, there may not be any need for a continuous Internet connection, as s/he can access it in the neighborhood café for free while having a coffee every once in a while.

- Transition to digital communication:

While most of us already use cell phones and even email, it may be less common to use videoconferencing and chat means for substituting face-to-face communications. The transition to ICT-based communication is usually easier, because it does not really involve a new practice that we need to learn, but we only have to get used to the location and time flexibility it provides.

4. *Time Management*

While time management can be plainly defined as the management of time in a way that makes the most out of it, the essence of it is to first define goals and outcomes, and the physical actions required to accomplish them, and finally to plan the process in the time required to manage the actions to complete these goals. There are a variety of principles, systems and approaches that can be used for time management, and ICT devices and software can greatly facilitate each step of this entire process. The simplest time management tools are electronic calendar software that can be run on smartphones, PDAs, PDA-phones and larger laptop and desktop computers. These software have various integrated tools that can be used to maintain daily, weekly, monthly and yearly calendars with activity logs, action plans and prioritized to-do lists. They often also have integrated communications and contact management capacities so that email and phone calls can be directly linked to the contact lists and calendar and action plans. There are also a variety of project management, goal setting and mind mapping software that can greatly enhance your time management and life management capabilities. Because these tools are most commonly shared on and operated from different ICT devices such as your cellular PDA-phone, laptop computer and desktop computer, they work best when integrated wirelessly over the Internet with specialized software that synchronizes files between devices that are Internet-capable. Exchange servers are one example of such software that synchronizes calendar, email and note data between all devices that are set up to communicate in this fashion through the Internet. Many Internet email services also offer time management tools that are integrated with the online email service so that you can maintain all your appointments, task plans and contacts online, and access them from wherever you have an Internet connection. Defeating procrastination is, of course, one of the most essential steps toward effective time management, and the flexible workstyle that is enabled by ICT is particularly susceptible to procrastination. I have outlined several strategies in Chapters 10 and 18 to counteract this time-killing behavior.

- What works best for me?

If you travel frequently, you'll definitively need a mobile handheld device like a PDA or PDA-phone with integrated time management capabilities. If, on the other hand, you are mostly stationed at home, you can simply use relevant software on your main computer. If your work tasks are complex and involve several partners, tasks, milestones and so on, then you may want to consider specialized project management software. If your work tasks only involve deadlines and appointments, your email software should have adequate calendar and contact list capabilities for you needs.

- Transition from paper-based time management:

Because ICT-based time management tools provide many more functionalities than the classical paper-based calendars, I would suggest transitioning at all costs, regardless of whether you want to remain paper-based with most of your activities. When transferring your contacts into the electronic format, it is easiest to use a laptop or desktop computer with a regular keyboard and then synchronize this data with your smaller handheld devices such as a PDA-phone. Make sure to back up your calendar and contact lists. Use a free Internet-based service to maintain all your calendar appointments, tasks and contact lists safely online.

5. *Document and file archiving*

Once you've gone paperless, you'll have to make sure that your electronic files are archived in a way that they can be accessed when you need them and that they are safe, both from unwanted eyes and from being lost. Archiving and backing up our files is one of the most important paperless practices, because technology can malfunction and lead to the loss of essential work and personal documents. When our files are regularly backed up and archived in an appropriate manner, we achieve a document loss prevention safety level that is much superior to what can be achieved with paper-based documents, even if you have a bank vault available for storage. This is because you can store digital copies, or backups, of your files at multiple locations such as your home desktop, laptop and on a backup hard drive. You will have to decide how to name documents in a way that can allow for easy retrieval and how to organize them on the hard drive or server. While the organization may seem less important once files have been named appropriately, it will still help tremendously when you search for something with a forgotten file name, or if you simply don't remember if the file exists at all.

- Naming files:

There are a variety of ways and rules for naming files. Whichever way you choose to name your files, make sure you use a system that enables you to figure out what that file is simply by the name. Use meaningful file names for your documents. A file name such as Summary is less useful than Robinson_Canton_10_2004. A file name should ideally contain keywords or letters that the user and collaborators can use to gain an understanding of what these files are.

- Organizing files:

You can create directories and subdirectories that follow the same logic of organizing files in file cabinets. When converting to a paperless system, it may simply be best to use the same organization structure as in the file cabinet system. In general, you'll have a broad category folder, such as "My Documents," and within this you'll have subfolders containing additional subcategories. In Part I we talked about the messy traditional office desktop with paper piles that contain information of organizational value. While this mode of file and document organization may seem impossible to mimic on a computer, software is currently being developed that will mimic this way of organizing documents as files in piles on a virtual desktop. The transition phase from paper to paperless will be particularly intense with archiving and backing up activities. It is essential to have settled on a naming and file organization system from the beginning so that all documents end up in the right place.

- Synchronizing files and data:

It's very important to pay attention to the synchronization between your ICT devices. Eventually, you'll find yourself working with at least two to three different ICT devices. A common combination is a desktop computer, a laptop computer, and a PDA-phone. You will be working on the same file on these three devices; when at home you'll use the desktop and when traveling the laptop, while the PDA-phone may be used when the laptop is inconvenient for the location. A problem that often arises is that we end up with different copies and versions of the same file (text) on these different devices, and if we are dealing with multiple files, the complexity can become confusing. The danger is that we'll lose track of which file represents the most recent version, and on which device it is residing. Ideally, a system should be in place that synchronizes the versions of documents between the different devices in such a way that when a change is made on one device, this change is automatically also made on the same file on all devices. In this way you will always have the most recent version available regardless of which device you are using. This synchronization can be done manually by making sure that you always transfer the most recent file versions to all your devices after you have made changes to it; this can be done through a flash memory stick, or, even better, by e-mailing it to yourself. In this way, it will end up in all devices that have email capabilities. But there is also specialized software that synchronizes files between devices that are Internet capable. Exchange servers are one example of software that synchronizes calendar, email and note data between all devices that are set up to communicate their calendar and email software in this fashion through the Internet. The method of choice for file and general data synchronization will depend on the type of work tasks; if you are an intense user of word processing files and frequently work on the same files using all your ICT devices, then specialized synchronization software will be appropriate for this. If you only rarely work on text documents using more than one device, then it will work perfectly well to simply use email or a flash memory to transfer this between the devices.

- Backing up:

Backing up your hard drive is essential and the paperless system will only make sense when this is done regularly. There are several ways of doing this, and the most common is to use an external hard drive that is connected to your computer through a USB cable. There are both stationary and portable high capacity hard drives available on the market. It may be wise to maintain a backup at different geographic locations, in case a disaster such as fire of flooding occurs. You can use specific software that automatically backs up the computer hard drive at a pre-determined interval on to another hard drive. One practical and flexible way to back up files safely is to use a remote archiving service through the Internet. These companies rent space, in gigabytes, and enable both manual and automatic backups through the Internet. The advantages of these systems are that they are safe from natural disasters and enable the access of files from wherever you have Internet access through a username and password.

- What works best for me?

Your method for naming and organizing (archiving) files will be most efficient if you use a naming system that contains relevant information for each document and file. How you organize your files in a computer should facilitate finding them when you need them, as well as provide logical structure that helps to organize your work. The method for synchronizing and backing up files will largely depend on your intensity of use, the importance of your documents, how many different ICT devices you plan to use for working on your documents and your required degree mobility, and if you need the ability to back up your files from multiple locations.

- Transition from paper-based archiving:

The most labor intensive part of this transition is always in the beginning, when you need to convert all your paper-based documents into digital formats. Here you can use a scanner with an autoloader to gradually scan all your documents. For small businesses and organizations it may be more effective to use a dedicated service as well as software. Scanning books to PDF format is a tedious process and you may have to decide if you really need them all in a digital form.

6. *Information gathering & research*

In the paper-based era, information was gathered in libraries, from books, journals, magazines and microfilms. The Internet has changed all that, and the large academic libraries in which scientific journals used to be stored have lost their importance, while most articles can be found through various databases on the World Wide Web as downloadable files. Data mining and research for information has changed, and now we can do a web search with specific keywords to find an unlimited number of resources. In fact, one of the difficulties that data mining faces today is to sort out irrelevant from relevant data and information. The way we search for information is essential for a successful retrieval of the most relevant sources and the various Internet –based search engines provide instructions on how to target relevant information in your search.

7. *Security*

The unprecedented flexibility in document and file identification, copying, and dispersal offered by paperless systems poses certain security risks, as electronic documents may fall into the wrong hands. There is a variety of software, readily available on the market, for direct purchase and download, that enable cyber spying. These cyber spy programs can retrieve passwords, email messages, Internet and chat history—in general, everything that was typed onto any one computer. Some of these programs can monitor computer activity remotely and send a report with the relevant information to the spy's email address at regular intervals. Our interactions and exchange of information with friends, colleagues, family, shops, financial institutions and any entity on the Internet is therefore vulnerable to interception and for falling into the wrong hands, and the consequences can be very severe when that happens.

The best ways to protect against such events are:

- The use of an up to date and good anti-virus program that can search your computer and incoming email messages for spy and other malicious software.
- A software and hardware firewall that will stop unwanted "visitors" from getting in. A good computer firewall will also prevent critical information from leaving your computer.
- Anti-virus, firewall and even the operating system, and other software with security patches, should be updated frequently.
- When you delete a file it can be retrieved again from the invisible sections of the hard drive by using specific software. It may therefore be safe to use specific eraser software to clean the hard drive from previously deleted files and thereby make them irretrievable.
- Use strong passwords of at least eight characters that include lower and upper case letters, numbers and special characters. The password should be changed frequently and you may even want to consider a password protected screen saver that basically will lock your computer after a certain period of inactivity. This may be particularly relevant for computers located in places where other people have access to it, and laptops that can be easily stolen. Many

of the newer ICT devices, and in particular laptops, have integrated fingerprint readers that can link the password for the particular computer and applications and web services with your fingerprint. In this way, you won't need to remember several different passwords, or type them in each time you need to access the service.

- Destroy the hard disk before you dispose of your outdated computer system.

Laptops and external hard drives are particularly susceptible to theft, and this poses a serious risk when sensitive information is stored on such devices. You can prevent the theft of your laptop by securing it to something immobile with a special laptop chain, or lock. Another laptop security measure is a password-protected disk encryption system that protects the data or renders it unreadable without the password. The best safety measure, however, is not to leave it at locations where it could be easily stolen.

- What works best for me?

Your choice and level of investment on computer security systems will largely depend on the sensitivity of your work; if you work with highly confidential material, you'll need to make sure that your system is very secure. It will also depend on how much Internet-based communication you will use and how much interaction with the World Wide Web you will engage in; these are the main sources of viruses and other malicious software.

8. *Powering your paperless ICT*

ICT devices and systems rely on electronics and therefore paperless practices are largely dependent on the availability of electricity. Any disruption in electricity supply will result in the discontinuation of work, and in some cases also the loss of information. Desktop devices are mostly powered from the electricity grid, while portable devices rely on batteries, which can either be purchased fully charged, or be charged from the electricity grid. Important considerations for devices that for the most part are directly powered from the electricity grid are the quality and reliability of the electricity supply and the cost. Some ICT devices can be particularly sensitive to abrupt power disruptions and voltage fluctuations (surges and spikes). Power surge protector devices that will stabilize the voltage and also provide power through batteries in the case of a power outage can be used to prevent damage and work disruption. If ICT devices that are powered directly from the electricity grid need to be relocated to a different world region one may need an electricity voltage transformer and plug convertor to ensure compatibility with a foreign electricity grid system and sockets. One can save significantly on reduced electricity consumption by adjusting power consumption settings and setting the computer to enter a stand-by mode when not used.

One should have high capacity reserve batteries available and set the power consumption to an energy conserving level to ensure extended continuous operation of mobile battery powered devices. Power consumption can be decreased by switching off certain functions such as the wireless antennae and the Bluetooth function, and lowering the brightness of the screen. When working off the battery, save documents frequently to prevent loss in case of a sudden power disruption. Having all the appropriate socket convertors is also important to enable re-charging when an electricity source, such as the regular grid or a car is available, even if only temporarily.

For devices that only require low power consumption one can use solar powered and even mechanically (manually) powered battery chargers and thereby be independent of the availability of an electricity grid.

18. HOW TO STAY COMMITTED WHILE ENJOYING PAPERLESS FREEDOM

The ICT enabled freedom to perform tasks in a location and time independent manner will inevitably present many tempting opportunities for procrastination. Fortunately there are many ways to stay on course and not become a victim to procrastination and I will outline some basic measures one can take to maintain productivity while enjoying paperless freedom.

A first step to avoiding procrastination is recognizing the reasons for procrastination and their different forms of expressions. The next step is to promptly gain control before these expressions become habit and steal valuable time from reaching your goals.

Some of the most commons causes of procrastination are:

- waiting for the right mood and time to perform a task
- a lack of clear goals
- underestimating the level of difficulty and the time required for the task
- a lack of clear standards for the expected outcomes of the task
- a feeling that the task is imposed on us
- a feeling that the task and its standards for outcome are to ambiguous
- a lack of adequate decision making skills
- a fear of failure or success
- an obsession with perfectionism

We can recognize the following most common signs of procrastination:

- postponing our most important tasks until later
- performing our tasks at the last minute or late
- waiting for a special mood to start the task or another time to start the task
- hesitation about making decisions

There are many strategies to overcome procrastination, and here are some of the most effective:

Develop interest in the work task.

We always prioritize things we find interesting at the expense of the less interesting things. We're more likely to get things done on time if we can develop excitement and interest for the task we have to do. Not only will that counteract procrastination, but it will also make that task more pleasant to perform. Convincing yourself of the importance of your work, both from a personal and a professional point of view, will always help in developing excitement for it. You can, for instance, tell yourself how important this is for your company and think about the earnings this work is going to get you and all the wonderful things you can spend it on and the security it will bring you.

It may sometimes be impossible to develop excitement and interest for a certain task, and in that case you will have to work on it whether you like it or not. The best way to deal with something unpleasant is to confront it; accept its presence and necessity and then simply deal with it. In these cases it may help to remind yourself of the earnings and job security that will result from the completion of such tasks. ICT can be used to make certain boring and unpleasant activities more pleasant (see Chapters 3). Finally, it will only be possible to deal with procrastination if you acknowledge it as a serious problem.

Make a plan and organize your tasks visually.

Development of a visual map or representation of your goals—in order of priority—can be a very powerful way to avoid procrastination. This can be done either with a calendar on your PDA or computer, with each task and milestone indicated at specific dates and times. You can also use more specialized mind mapping and project management software to make visual maps or charts in which the duration of tasks, the effort required by them, deadlines and other information can be presented. Always keep a list of the tasks that have to be done to fulfill your professional or personal commitments. Then determine the importance, effort and estimated duration for each of these tasks. According to those measures, place these tasks in a time frame starting with the most important tasks, and then adhere to that plan.

To estimate the required time and difficulty of future tasks more realistically, it can be helpful to compare the estimated time to the actual time after you've completed a task. It's essential to establish milestones and deadlines for each task in order to realistically monitor your progress in a time scale. Make contingency time available in the plan for the unexpected events than may cause delays in task completion. Larger tasks can be chunked down into several sub-tasks with their own deadlines; this will greatly facilitate their completion. If you find yourself completing certain tasks faster than expected, you can either revise the plan or convert the surplus time into leisure time. If a task turns out to require more time, or unexpected changes occur, then revise the scheme. Project and mapmaker software can greatly help with the organization of tasks in a time scheme.

The most difficult part of performing a certain task is its initiation. The solution for this is to not put tasks off until the last minute and just get started. Once you actually start working on a task, you will often find that it's easier than you expected, and you're going to complete it quickly.

Become accountable for task completion.

If you work for a company or organization, it's very likely that your employer will request—or require--reports on task progression. If you work freelance, you are more vulnerable to procrastination, because you don't have an immediate supervisor to check on your progress and directly request task completion. In that case, you can simply ask someone—a friend or business partner, perhaps—to do the job of a supervisor and monitor, remind and request reports of your task completion progress. Another way may be to send a progress reports to your clients periodically with a predicted completion date. Another way to maintain the necessary work pace for task completion can be to become visible, either directly in your working environment or through a webcam in your work space. In this way, those to whom you have made yourself accountable can immediately monitor your activity and prompt you when you engage in unsanctioned activities. By sharing your task plans or maps with those to whom you have made yourself accountable, you will also help them to keep track of your progress. Finally, all electronic calendars have both visual and audible reminder systems that can be set to frequently remind you of approaching task deadlines.

Chose the right environment for task completion and avoid distractions.

Procrastination can often result from distractions that make it difficult to focus on the actual task. It is therefore important to choose an environment that won't provide such distractions. Working in front of the TV, for instance, can create the temptation to relocate attention to other things than the actual task. You may also want to turn off your phone ringer and even email in order to avoid distractions.

Remind yourself of and document the consequences of procrastination.

Procrastination always leads to negative consequences such as compromised reputation, lower earnings, loss of projects and threats from clients or supervisors. Whenever you find yourself procrastinating, remind yourself of such consequences with real past examples, and urgency for task completion will soon hit you.

Reward yourself upon task completion.

Procrastination can be avoided by simply deciding to reward yourself for getting tasks done in time.

It is obviously in the employer's interest to counteract procrastination of employees, and this may become particularly challenging when employees are working outside of their immediate supervision. There are several ways to ensure work is being done when employees are working outside of the office without compromising their location and time flexibility. Some of these are outlined in Chapters 10 and 13.

19. SPREAD THE PAPERLESS WORK PHILOSOPHY

To fully enjoy a paperless work- and lifestyle in which we get tasks done faster and in a more location and time flexible manner through a seamless use of ICT devices and software it will be necessary for our collaborators, employers, clients, colleagues and others to also become paperless. If not, we will continuously have to deal with compatibility issues, and we'll spend too much time and effort converting electronic documents to paper and vice versa. This becomes particularly important at the workplace, as it would be impossible to integrate seamlessly into a work team that mainly uses paper for its projects. Imagine how you would have to scan all incoming documents and print all outgoing documents when working with this team. This would not make much sense—it would be better for every team member to go paperless.

To make our paperless life better and more fulfilling we have to spread the paperless work philosophy further. Remember that the battle will always start in the mind. First we have to convince our intended partners in paperlessness that it will greatly benefit them, and that it is feasible. Use the arguments outlined in this book and elsewhere, and tailor them to the specific situation. If you need to convince your corporate upper management to implement paperless workstyles, you'll need to show them how it will benefit business operations, profits and employee satisfaction. If you need to convince your freelance co-worker, you may need to highlight the benefits of flexibility and more free time. The best way to convince is always to demonstrate the paperless style and its advantages practically—by being paperless yourself. People around you will become curious when they see the lack of paper piles, or when they see you using a tablet to take notes. This is the opportunity to tell them about your clutter-free life, and how you enjoy being on top of your business and how you benefit from the flexibilities, productivity and free time that paperless workstyles bring you. You can tell them more about how you became paperless and even recommend this book for reading. Sooner or later, the world will become paperless, and early adopters will have a greater chance to shape and influence their futures and enjoy its advantages from an early stage.

20. STAY TUNED TO THE PAPERLESS FUTURE

Because paperless practices are directly and intimately dependent on ICT, which in turn is evolving at a fast pace, we can expect many advances to occur (even in the near future) that will alter the way we do things. Fortunately, these changes will make paperless practices better, easier and more efficient. They will enable a better simulation of paper and make it easier for us to go paperless. In order to enjoy these new advances in technology we will have to keep an eye on them and occasionally update our knowledge and know-how about our ICT devices and software. However, once we have set up the paperless system and learned how to operate it, the updating should be straightforward when we become aware of the new models and versions.

Updating will mostly involve acquiring a new model with a higher capacity and this may not necessarily change the actual paperless work practice, but only make it more efficient. An example is a new scanner with a faster scanning time and better resolution; this will allow us to spend less time on scanning paper documents. Occasionally, a disruptive technology will appear, radically changing the way we do certain practices. An example of such was the development of speech recognition software that basically enabled the generation of typed text through speech.

There are a variety of information sources that one can use to stay tuned with the ever evolving paperless technologies, such as online electronics and office equipment magazines. The Paperless Joy Blog (http://enjoypaperless.blogspot.com/) and Digital Life Artist Inc. (www.digitallifeartist.com) websites provide up to date information on paperless technologies, trends and work practices for variety of situations, and are therefore relevant sources for staying up to date with the paperless environment.

GLOSSARY

1,2,3,4G: Short for different generations (G) of wireless telephone technology.

ADSL: Stands for "Asymmetric Digital Subscriber Line" and is a form of DSL that has different download and upload speeds.

Anti-virus: Software that find, blocks and removes malicious virus software from a computer.

Apple: Apple is the company that manufactures Macintosh computers. The Apple product line includes Power Macs, PowerBooks, iMacs, iBooks, the portable multimedia player iPod, iPhone, and a variety of software programs, such as iTunes, iPhoto, iMovie, and iDVD.

Applet: A Java program that is embedded in an HTML page. Java applets are not allowed to access certain resources, such as files, modems, printers, etc., on the computer.

ASCII: Stands for "American Standard Code for Information Interchange" and is the defacto world-wide standard for the code numbers used by computers to represent all the upper and lower-case Latin letters, numbers, punctuation, etc. There are 128 standard ASCII codes each of which can be represented by a 7 digit binary number: 0000000 through 111111.

Audiobook: A book that has been recorded as spoken words and can therefore be "read" through listening.

Backup: A copy on a CD disk or external hard drive of files from a PC's hard disk. A backup is used in case the hard disk file(s) are erased or damaged.

Bandwidth: A measurement, in bits per second, of how much data that can be sent through an Internet connection.

Bit: A bit is the smallest unit of information that a computer uses.

BITNET: Stands for "Because It's Time Network" and is a network of educational sites separate from the Internet. E-mail is however freely exchanged between the Internet and BITNET.

Blog: Name derived from web log and is a journal posted on the World Wide Web, and frequently updated through blogging by a "blogger." Blogs are usually arranged in chronological order with the most recent additions at the top.

Bluetooth: A technology, developed and licensed by The Bluetooth Special Interest Group, which is used to enable communication between ICT devices through wireless short-range radio frequency personal area networks (PANs).

Boot: The startup procedure for a computer when the operating system is initiated and loaded to prepare the computer for running software applications. Startup instructions are derived from the boot disk on the hard disk.

Broadband: A high-speed multiple channel capacity data transmission, through a single cable, which is used for Internet access. Types of broadband connections are cable modems (use the same connection as cable TV) and DSL modems (use your existing phone line). Wireless broadband connections have also been launched in recent years.

Browser: A software which is used to interact with, or browse, the World Wide Web on the Internet.

Bug: Usually a small defect in a software that makes it malfunction.

Cache: A type of memory used to make a computer work faster.

CDMA: Stands for "Code Division Multiple Access" and is a combination of 2nd- (or 2G) and 3rd (or 3G) -generation cellular phone networks. Data transmission involves conversion of analog to digital signals.

CD-ROM: A disk with the same format as an audio CD which is used for storing digital computer information.

Cellular phone: Also called cell phone, mobile phone, mobile or wireless, is a portable ICT device that is used for mobile wireless communication and connection to the landline-based telephone network through a network of base stations. In addition to telephone communication functions, some cell phone devices can also enable other services such as access to the Internet, email and text messaging.

Client: A software program that is used to contact and obtain data from a Server software program on another computer, often across a great distance. Each Client program is designed to work with one or more specific kinds of Server programs, and each Server requires a specific kind of Client. A Web Browser is a specific type of Client.

Compact Disc: Abbreviated as CD, a compact disc is a polycarbonate disc with one or more metal layers capable of storing digital information. The music industry uses these types of discs to store digital recordings and the CD-ROMs are used to store computer data. These types of compact disc are read-only, which means that once the data has been recorded onto them, they can only be read, or played. The rewritable types can allow one to erase and re-record data on the disc.

Cookie: Information sent by a Web Server to a Web Browser to be saved on the recipient device. The cookie's purpose is to send information back to the Server whenever the browser makes additional communications with the Server. This information can be login or registration information, online "shopping cart" information, user preferences, etc. This information will allow the server to customize the data that is sent back to the user.

CPU: Stands for "Central Processing Unit" and can be considered the PC's central part, or brain. A CPU, or processor, refers to a class of logic machines that can execute computer programs.

CRT: Stands for cathode ray tube is a type of monitor that is based on a vacuum tube containing an electron gun (a source of electrons) and a fluorescent screen.

DAP: Stands for "Digital Audio Player" and are usually small portable devices used for storing and playing digital music which is stored on either flash based memory cards or hard drives and usually transmits the audio to the listener through earphones.

Desktop Computer: A stand-alone non-mobile computer also called personal computer (PC). As the name indicates, a desktop computer can fit on a desk and it has traditionally consisted of four integrated and interconnected parts; the computer, the monitor, a keyboard and a mouse. The styles of desktop computers have evolved in the past years and come in different formats and configurations. The integrated small form factor models in which the computer and monitor are integrated in one case have become popular. The following are the main features and advantages of desktops computers.

- The ability to integrate different components (i.e. monitors, keyboard, hard drive) at the customer's choice into the final product.
- The standardization of parts that makes them less costly and the sometimes higher durability as a result of not having to miniaturize the various components as in the case of laptop computers.
- Desktops computers frequently also have a variety of standardized expansion slots which can be used for connections to peripheral components. This means that a desktop can be customized and upgraded to a greater extent than laptops.
- Desktop computers can be opened and modified (i.e. upgraded with larger memory) by the user since the procedures for (dis-)assembly tend to be simple and standardized. In fact many users build their own desktop computers by purchasing and assembling the various components of desired specifications.
- The desktop computer has often larger and more ergonomic keyboard and mouse, and larger monitors, and is hence easier to work with.
- The desktop computer is powered through the electricity grid and power consumption is therefore not as critical compared to a laptop

computer which is powered by a rechargeable battery. This allows for the use of more powerful and therefore eats producing processors compared to laptop computers.

Dictaphone: A handheld digital audio recorder and player that can be used to take speech notes or interviews. The sound files can be transferred to a computer for storage or conversion to typed text through speech recognition software.

Digitized Work Practice: A work practice that previously was done through the use of paper or face to face interaction but now is performed through the use of paperless ICT.

Dispersed Work Team: A team of co-workers that that perform work tasks across time, space, and organizational boundaries with ICT. Also called virtual teams or Geographically Dispersed Teams (GDT).

Domain Name: The unique name that identifies an Internet based World Wide Web site.

DOS: Stand for "Disk Operating System" and is the original operating system used for PCs.

Download: The transfer of data from another computer to the computer being used. It is the opposite of upload.

Driver: A program that enables a computer to use certain peripheral ICT devices.

DSL: Stands for "Digital Subscriber Line" and is a method for transferring data rapidly over regular phone lines.

DVI: Stands for "Digital Visual (or Video) Interface" and is a socket used to connect external monitors to an ICT device such as a computer.

eBook: Refers to a digital version of a paper book, as well as the electronic reading device such as for example the Kindle, Rocket eBook or Pocket PC.

eBook Reader: A device that can display digital versions of books, e-paper magazines or other types of electronic documents, through electronic paper, or electronic ink, technology which mimic the appearance of ordinary ink on paper. Electronic paper reflects light like ordinary paper and can display the text or images indefinitely without consuming electricity, and power is only needed when the page is turned. Electronic paper can only display static mages or text, but not moving images, and is therefore most suitable for reading texts. The biggest advantages of eBook readers are the small size, low weight, low electricity consumption and the fact that they can hold hundreds of books in their memory. As such, these devices can make hundreds of books or documents available for reading at any location without the need for electricity. An eBook reader is therefore a great companion on long flights or other types of travel, but also at home or at office. Some eBook readers can directly connect to eBook stores on the Internet through a computer of wirelessly. Some e-book readers can also automatically download daily news papers and magazines wirelessly and thereby replace daily news papers.

EDGE: Stands for "Enhanced Data for Global Evolution" and is an enhanced version of GPRS that enables two to three times faster data transfer.

Electronic Mail: Also called email or e-mail and is a messages sent from one computer to another through the Internet.

Electronic Paper: Also called electronic ink and is display technology that displays visual content with a paper-like look and only consumes energy when the image is changed.

Ethernet: A method of networking (connecting) computers in a local area network (LAN).

Fingerprint Reader: An identification device, mostly based on an optical sensor, that capture a digital image of a finger print as the finger is placed or slid over it. This image is then compared and matched to a stored print to verify the identity of the user. These types of devices are frequently integrated into laptops or externally linked to a computer through a USB connection and monitor the logon procedure thereby replacing the necessity to type in a password.

Fire Wall: A computer firewall protects a networked server or client machine (personal computer) from entry by unauthorized users that could cause damage to the software or stored data.

Flash Memory: A non-volatile (does not require power to maintain stored information) electronic memory with no moving parts that can be erased and reprogrammed.

Folder: Also called directory and is a sub-division of a computer's hard disk into which files can be placed and organized.

Format: Hard disks have to be electronically prepared prior to use by a process called formatting.

FTP: Stands for "File Transfer Protocol" and is a method of transferring files between two computers through the Internet.

GIF: Stands for "Graphic Interchange Format" and is a file format for images files.

Gigabyte: The equivalent of 1000 Megabytes.

GPRS: Stands for "General Packet Radio Services" and is a packet-based wireless communication service that enables data transfer rates up to 114 Kbps. GPRS is usually used for cell phone or laptop connections to the Internet.

GPS: Stands for "Global Positioning System" and is used to pin point a user's precise geographic location on a mobile ICT device through satellite signals.

Graphics Card: The component inside a computer that is responsible for creating the images on the screen.

GUI: Stands for "Graphical User Interface" and enables users to interact and navigate with information on their computer display using a mouse or other pointing device to point, click, and drag data and icons around on the screen, instead of typing in words and phrases as commands.

Hard Disk: Also called hard drive (HDD) is a sealed disk or non-volatile (does not require power to maintain stored information) memory device which stores data, such as programs and information, magnetically on rapidly rotating metallic platters. HDDs are mostly used internally in computers and a variety of other devices such as video recorders, portable media players, PDAs, digital cameras and video game consoles. They also exist as external and portable devices for large-scale, reliable storage.

Hardware: Touchable objects such as disks, disk drives, display screens, keyboards, printers and memory cards. Software is in contrast untouchable and has no substance. An analogue to computer hardware and software are books where pages and ink represent the hardware, while the letters and words, provide the overall meaning of the book and represent the software. Computer software cannot function without the hardware and conversely a computer without the software can be viewed as a book without words.

Headset: A wearable set of headphones and microphone that connects to a computer, cell phone or portable media and enables audio communication.

Hit: A hit refers to a single request from a World Wide Web browser for a single item (or page) from a World Wide Web server.

Home Page: The World Wide Web page that a browser will display when it starts up, or the main World Wide Web page of a website.

Host: A computer on a network that serve as a repository for services available to other computers on the network.

Hotspot: An area where Wi-Fi enabled ICT devices can connect to the Internet through a wireless Local Area Network (WLAN) which often is free of charge.

HTML: Stands for "HyperText Markup Language" and is the coding language used to create Hypertext documents for the use on the World Wide Web. HTML files are viewed using a "Web Browser".

HTTP: Stands for "HyperText Transfer Protocol" and is used for moving hypertext files across the Internet. HTTP is the most used and important protocol used on the World Wide Web.

Hypertext: Any text that contains links to other documents or World Wide Web sites.

Icon: A small image or picture on a computer screen that is a symbol for folders, disks, peripherals, programs, etc..

ICT: The Information Technology Association of America (ITAA) has defined information technology (IT) in the electronic era as "the study, design, development, implementation, support or management of computer-based information systems, particularly software applications and computer hardware." If a process involves the use of computers and software to create, convert, store, manage, transmit and retrieve information securely in a paperless manner, then it is considered an IT process. Recently, the term has been broadened to include electronic forms of communication, giving us the term information and communications technology, or ICT.

IEEE 1394: Stands for "Institute of Electrical and Electronics Engineers Standard 1394" and is also called "Firewire" or "iLink" and is used for high throughput data transfer between ICT devices, similarly to USB connections.

IMAP: Stands for "Internet Message Access Protocol" and is gradually replacing POP as the main protocol used for communications between email clients and servers.

Internet: An international network of computers that provide services such as the World Wide Web and electronic mail.

Intranet: A private network within an organization that uses the same kinds of software that you would find on the Internet, but that is only available for internal use.

IP Number: Stands for "Internet Protocol Number" and is a unique number for every device connected to the Internet.

ISDN: Stands for "Integrated Services Digital Network" and is a method to transfer data over regular phone lines. ISDN can be used to connect to many different locations that also have ISDN.

ISP: Stands for "Internet Service Provider" and is an entity that provides access to the Internet.

Java: A network-oriented programming language used to build large, complex systems involving several different ICT devices that interact across networks such as transaction processing systems. Java programs called "Applets" can allow Web pages to include functions such as animations.

JPEG: Stands for "Joint Photographic Experts Group" and is an image file format.

Keyboard: An ICT peripheral device that enables input of data to a computer through typing.

Kilobyte: The equivalent to one thousand bytes.

Kindle: An electronic ink –based eBook reader marketed by Amazon.com.

LAN: Stands for "Local Area Network" and is a limited computer network within a home, office, or group of buildings. Ethernet and Wi-Fi are the two most common technologies to support a LAN.

Laptop Computer: Also called laptop, notebook or portable computer, is a battery powered mobile computer, which can range in weight from 2 to 18 pounds (1 to 8 kilograms), depending on size, materials, and other factors. Laptop computers can be powered both by an integrated or external rechargeable battery and from an external AC/DC adapter that is plugged into the electricity grid. Many laptop computers also have an integrated smaller battery to power the clock and other processes in the case power failure.

Laptop computers are built with similar, but miniaturized, components to their desktop counterparts and can perform the same functions. Some of these components have more efficient power consumption to allow for extended battery powering. The miniaturization and energy efficiency frequently renders laptop computer components less powerful and more expensive compared to desktop computer components. Laptop computers have integrated computer, monitor and keyboard, and a touchpad serve the role of the mouse. External keyboard, mouse and monitor can be connected to the laptop computer and thereby give it a more desktop-like operation at the cost of mobility. Laptop computers can be classified in different categories based on their size, weight and other features.

- The Thin-and-light laptop computer typically weight between 4 and 6 lb (1.8–2.7 kg) and have a screen of 12 to 14 inches (30–35 cm) diagonally.
- The mainstream laptop computers weight between 5 and 7 lb (2.3–3.2 kg) and have a screen size of 14.1 or 15.4 inches (35 or 39 cm) diagonally.
- The substantially larger and heavier desktop replacement lap top computers are not really suitable for placement on a lap. However, these powerful devices have the same computing specifications to desktop computers and are meant to be mainly used in a fixed location 17–20 inches (43–51 cm). Due to the desktop-like power consumption these laptop computers tend to have limited battery life. Desktop replacement computers are ideal for those who require high computing performance and large screen size while still enjoying mobility.

In sum, laptop computers are devices large enough to use the same software as a desktop machine, but small enough to enable mobility. Major advantages of laptop computers are mobility and flexibility.

Linux: An Open Source Unix-like operating system available for anyone to examine and change as long as they make their changes available to the public.

Login: The procedure used to connect to a computer system by providing user credentials such as username and password.

Mac OS: The operating system used to run Macintosh computers.

Macintosh: The name of the computers that are made by Apple Computer Inc. The first Macintosh was introduced in 1984 and was seen as a major innovation in computing ease-of-use. The Macintosh was the first personal computer to use a graphical user interface (GUI), which allowed the user to interact with the operating system by using a mouse to click and drag objects. Since 1984, Apple has continually revised and upgraded the Macintosh product line and now makes both laptop and desktop versions of the Macintosh, as well as portable media players and a variety of peripheral ICT devices. The Macintosh product line includes the following five different models.

- -Power Mac - the high-performance desktop computer for professionals.
- PowerBook - the high-performance laptop computer for professionals.
- iMac - the creatively designed consumer desktop computer.
- iBook - the laptop computer for students and home users.
- eMac - the all-in-one desktop computer for educators and entry-level consumers.

Macintosh computers run the Macintosh operating system, creatively named the "Mac OS."

Mail List: An automated system that enables users to send an e-mail message to an address from where this message is sent to all subscribers of the mail list.

Megabyte: The equivalent of one million bytes.

Megahertz: A measure of computer processor (CPU) speed. One megahertz equals one million cycles per second.

Megapixel: A measurement of image resolution which is equal to 1 million pixels.

Memory: Non volatile media used for the temporary storage of information while a computer is being used. RAM, ROM and Cache type memory exist.

Microprocessor: A microprocessor comprises all functions of a central processing unit (CPU) on an integrated circuit (IC).

Microsoft Reader: Microsoft Reader is a free software provided by Microsoft for reading eBooks.

Mirror: To mirror means to maintain an exact copy of a World Wide Web site or webpage as a "mirror site" at another location. This is done to provide more widespread access to the site.

Modem: Also called "Modulator" and "Demodulator" is a device that is used for enabling Internet access or fax by connecting a computer to a phone line.

Mouse: A pointing device connected to the computer used for moving items on the screen and executing commands with GUI software by dragging the mouse in on a plain surface.

MP3: Stands for "Moving Picture experts Group layer 3" and is a standard file format for compressed audio such as music. The compressing renders these files small and this allows for easy exchange through the Internet and a large number of MP3 music files can be stored on a DAP or portable media player.

Network: When two or more computers are connected to each other they represent a network. Networks enable the sharing of files and information between multiple ICT devices.

Newsgroup: A discussion group on the USENET.

OCR: Stands for "Optical Character Recognition" and is a software that converts text that has been scanned as an image into actual lettering.

Open Source Software: A software that has its underlying programming code available to users to enable them to read it, make changes to it, and build new versions of the software.

Operating System: The operating system (OS) is the basic software of a computer that manages interactions with and between a computer's resources such as the keyboard, screen, mouse, hard drive, disc drives and printers. The operating system also controls the allocation of memory and maintains an inventory of files and directories on the hard drive. Most ICT devices that operate software, such as mobile phones, PDAs, portable media players, game consoles and digital cameras use an operating system.

Parallel Port: A socket at the back of a computer used to connect external devices or peripherals such as printers.

Password: A password is a code or word used to gain access to restricted data on a computer network.

PC card: A device that is the same size as a thick credit card, for plugging into a PCMCIA (Stands for "Personal Computer Memory Card International Association") slot on laptop computers. The PC card can provide connection capability to memory, modems, hard disks and other peripherals.

PDA: Stands for "Personal Digital Assistant" and is a small, usually pocket-sized, mobile computer with a limited functionality. PDA's do not run desktop computer software while some applications have been made compatible with to desktop computers to enable exchange of documents and other type of information between these different devices. PDAs are mostly used as electronic calendars and address books, but can also run a variety of other software to be used for note taking, MP3 music players, audio book reading, specialized reference book reading, expense tracking and playing games. Some PDAs have wireless capabilities and can therefore also be used to receive and send e-mail, and browse the Internet.

PDA phone: A hand held computer, or PDA, with an integrated cell phone. In addition to all the standard wireless phone capabilities these devices have additional functionalities such as wireless calendar, email, contact and task lists, multimedia and word processing and multimedia software capabilities.

PDF: Stands for "Portable Document Format" and is a file format that was developed by Adobe Systems to represent a document in a way that is independent of the software, hardware and operating system that was used to create it.

Peripheral: Any ICT device that is connected externally to a computer such as printers, scanners and modems.

Pixel: Thousands of pixels make up the image on the screen as tiny dots.

Plug-in: A software that provides additional features to another software.

POP: Stands for "Post Office Protocol" and refers to a protocol used to retrieve e-mail from a remote mail server.

Port: Refers to a connection from where information goes into or out of a computer.

Portable Media Payer: Is a DAP with additional capabilities for image viewing and video playing.

Posting: A single message entered into a network communications system.

Printer: A device that can generate paper hard copies of documents stored in an electronic form. A local printer is attached through a cable to a computer which serves as a document source while a network printer can produce hardcopies for any user on a network through its built-in network interfaces. Some printers can directly connect to flash memory sticks or digital cameras for printing. Multi function printer devices are printers with integrated scanner and telephone – fax machine in a single unit and can be used for additional tasks including photocopying. Based on the printing technology, there are two main types of printers; laser and ink-jet. The laser printer can rapidly produce high quality text and graphics on plain paper and uses a xerographic printing process where the image is produced by the direct scanning of a laser beam across the printer's photoreceptor. The ink-jet printer relies on the deposition of tiny ink droplets onto the paper or any other media through a replaceable cartridge. Some ink-jet printers have multiple colors and can also be used for printing images on photographic paper. Most printers are desktop units powered by the electricity grid, while smaller portable printers also exist.

QWERTY: The first 6 letters on an English-language keyboard and indicate this type of standard keyboard layout.

RAM: Stands for "Random Access Memory" and is the main temporary memory used while the computer is working.

Read-only: A document which can be displayed but not modified or deleted.

Reading Device: A hardware used to read eBooks.

Resolution: The number of dots or pixels per area unit (square inch or square cm) used to create the screen image or print image.

Roaming: Roaming in wireless telecommunications refers to the extension of connectivity service in a location outside of the registered service location. Roaming is the ability to make and receive voice calls, or access other services, when traveling outside the geographical coverage area of the home network, by using a visited network.

ROM: Stands for "Read Only Memory" and is a type of memory with the information needed by the PC that cannot be changed.

Router: A computer software that handles the connection between packet-switched networks. Routers look at the source and destination addresses of the packets passing through them and decide on which route to send them on.

RSS: Stands for "Rich Site Summary" and are World Wide Web feed formats that are used to publish frequently updated content of for instance blog entries, news headlines, and podcasts in a standardized format.

Satellite telephone: Also called satphone and is a mobile phone that can connect to the telephony network through satellites and coverage may therefore include the entire Earth or only specific regions depending on the service. Satellite phones are significantly larger, heavier and more expensive than regular cell phones, and are therefore mostly used in remote areas where cell phone services are unavailable.

Scanner: A device that converts printed images, printed text, or handwriting, or a flat object into a digital image. The most common scanner is the desktop flatbed scanner. A variety of specialized scanners, such as the hand-held scanners and business card and receipt scanners also exist. Most scanners are directly connected to a computer onto which the scanned image is transferred. Some scanners are equipped with autoloaders that enables dual side scanning of many pages in an automatic fashion.

SDSL: Stands for "Symmetric Digital Subscriber Line" and is an Internet connection version of DSL where the upload speeds and download speeds are the same.

Search Engine: An application used to search the Internet for information available on the World Wide Web.

Security Certificate: Information that is used by the Internet browser to establish a secure connection.

Serial Port: A socket at the back of a PC for connecting peripherals. The serial ports have largely become substituted with the USB ports.

Server: A computer or device that performs service applications on a network for connected clients without the need for human direction. Common servers are e-mail servers, file servers and World Wide Web servers.

SIM Card: Stands for "subscriber identity module" and is a removable integrated circuit card that can securely store the cell phone subscriber identification information to allow users to change phones by simply removing the SIM card from one to another cellular phone.

Smartphone: A hand held device with wireless telephony capabilities and simple computing and multimedia capabilities that enable time management functions. The computing capabilities of a smartphone are less advanced compared to the PDA phone which is a true handheld computer.

Software: A program, documentation or procedures, that a computer uses to perform specific tasks. Computers use three main categories of software.

- -Application software such as time management software and word processors, which are used for productive tasks.
- System software such as operating systems, which interface with hardware to provide the necessary services for application software.
- Middleware, which co-ordinates and controls distributed systems.

Spam: Spamming is an inappropriate marketing strategy that involves the use of a mailing list, or USENET or other networked communications system to send the same marketing message to a large number of recipients who did not request it.

Stylus: A pen that is used for digital hand writing on hand held ICT devices equipped with touch screens.

Tablet Computer: A laptop computer featuring a touch screen interface and a stylus, plus handwriting recognition software. Tablet computers are the size of a notebook and the input of text can be done through handwriting or tapping on a virtual keyboard directly on the screen with the stylus. Some tablet computers, also called tablet PCs or convertibles, are a laptop with a touch screen that can be rotated 180 degrees and folded on top of the keyboard. The tablet PCs have identical features to the regular laptops with the additional tablet features.

TCP/IP: Stands for "Transmission Control Protocol/Internet Protocol" and is the suite of protocols that defines the Internet. TCP/IP software is usually included with every computer operating system to enable interaction with the Internet.

Telecommuting: Telecommuting is also referred as e-commuting, e-work or telework, and is an arrangement by which the daily commute to a central work place is replaced by telecommunication links. The employees enjoy a time and location flexible workstyle.

Telnet: A command and program that is used to login from one Internet site to another.

Template: A pre-formatted document that serves as a starting point for generating a new document with a standardized format.

Terabyte: The equivalent of 1000 gigabytes.

Terminal: A device, which at a minimum can consist of a keyboard and a display screen, allowing one to send commands for the operation of a remote computer.

TFT: Stands for "Thin Film Transistor" and is a type of high quality screen for laptop computers.

Trojan Horse: A malicious computer program that is usually hidden inside another program or file to trick potential users into running it. Unlike a virus it will usually not infect other programs.

UI: Stands for "User Interface" and refers to the communication between a computer and a user through a software.

Unix: A multi-user computer operating system that has built-in TCP/IP and is the most common operating system for Internet servers.

Upload: Transferring data (usually a file) from your computer to another computer, and is the opposite of download.

URL: Stands for "Uniform Resource Locator" and it the Internet–based address of a webpage.

USB: Stands for "Universal Serial Bus" and is a computer port used to connect peripherals (mouse, keyboard, game controllers, printers, scanners, and removable media drives, etc..) to a computer or between them.

USENET: Is a world-wide network of discussion groups, or newsgroups, that can share ideas and comments between hundreds of thousands of computers.

Virtual Team: Dispersed Work Team

Virus: A malicious program that makes copies of itself once transferred to a computer. Some viruses can display messages, install or delete other software or files and thereby cause damage. Viruses usually spread by attaching themselves to email messages, programs or files that are being communicated between users.

VoIP: Stands for "Voice-over-Internet protocol" and is a protocol used for transmission of voice through the Internet or other types of packet-switched networks. IP telephony, Internet telephony, voice over broadband, broadband telephony, and broadband phone use VoIP.

WAN: Stands for Wide Area Network and is a network that covers a larger area than a single building or enterprise.

Webcam: A small video camera that is linked to the World Wide Web through a computer and the Internet, and can be used for live video broadcasting. Webcams are often used for face-to-face interactions through instant messaging and video conferencing.

Wireless Router: A wireless network device that can function as a wireless LAN (Local Area Network).

Web Page: A document that can be viewed in a World Wide Web browser software.

Web Site: A World Wide Web site is a collection of World Wide Web pages and associated information such as images, sound, and video files, that are provided through a single World Wide Web server. The pages in a World Wide Web site share the same basic URL.

Webmaster: The person who is in charge of World Wide Web site maintenance and writes HTML for web pages, structures the Web, responds to e-mails about the Web site, and maintains the site up-to-date.

Wi-Fi: Stands for "Wireless Fidelity" and is a form of wireless data communication that is used for Internet, VoIP phone access, gaming, and network connectivity for ICT devices such as TVs, DVD players, and digital cameras.

Windows: One of the most commonly used operating system for personal computers (PC).

Wireless: The term is used to describe telecommunications by which electromagnetic waves transfer the signal over the communication path. Common wireless ICT devices are cellular phones, pagers, Global Positioning System (GPS), cordless computer peripherals, cordless telephone sets, satellite television and wireless local area networks (LAN).

Word Processor: Originally named "document preparation system" is a software that is used for the generation (including composition, editing, formatting, and possibly printing) of any sort of readable material.

World Wide Web: Also called the Web is a term that is frequently (incorrectly) used when referring to the Internet. It is a service available on the Internet and enables access to millions of pages through a system of links.

Worm: A virus that makes copies of itself and infects additional computers mainly through network connections. A worm can alter, install, or destroy files and programs.

Zip: A zip file (.zip) is a compressed or "zipped" file that takes up less hard drive space and takes less time to transfer to another computer. A zipped file needs to become unzipped to be used.

REFERENCES

(Organized according to the order of chapters)

INTRODUCTION

Definition of Information and Communication Technology (ICT). Wikipedia. Retrieved July 16, 2008, from http://en.wikipedia.org/wiki/Information_technology

1. *INFORMATION AND COMMUNICATION TECHNOLOGY (ICT) IS CHANGING OUR WORLD TOWARDS PAPERLESS*

Anne Wells Branscomb. The Economics of Information, 1994, Asis.org. Retrieved July 16, 2008, from: http://www.asis.org/Bulletin/Dec-94/branscom.html

Definition of Knowledge Economy. Businessdictionary.com. Retrieved July 16, 2008, from: http://www.businessdictionary.com/definition/knowledge-economy.html

2. *THE EVOLUTION OF ICT: PAPYRUS TO ELECTRONIC MEDIA*

Definition of Information and Communication Technology (ICT). Wikipedia. Retrieved July 16, 2008, from http://en.wikipedia.org/wiki/Information_technology

Jeremy G. Butler. A History of Information Technology and Systems, 1997, Retrieved August 4th, 2008, from: http://www.tcf.ua.edu/AZ/ITHistoryOutline.htm

History Of Paper. Retrieved August 4th, 2008, from: http://www.paperonline.org/history/history_frame.html

History Of Paper. Wikipedia. Retrieved July 16, 2008, from: http://en.wikipedia.org/wiki/Paper

Automatic Sequence Controlled Calculator (ASCC), also known as the Mark 1. Retrieved August 4th, 2008, from http://www-

03.ibm.com/ibm/history/exhibits/markI/markI_intro.html

The Telephone. Wikipedia. Retrieved August 3, 2008, from: http://en.wikipedia.org/wiki/Telephone

Cellular Telephony. Wikipedia. Retrieved August 3, 2008, from: http://en.wikipedia.org/wiki/Cellular_telephony

3. *IMPROVED QUALITY OF LIFE AND WORK—WITH ICT*

Alice Bredin. The Home Office Solution, 1998, John Wiley & Sons, Inc. USA.

Roger J. Callan. Circadian Rhythm and the Business Person, 1998, International Journal of ValueBased Management 11: 9–17.

Debra A. Dinnocenzo. 101 tips for Telecommuters, 1999, Berrett-Koehler Publishers, San Fransisco, USA.

Diana Fitzpatrick & Stephen Fishman. The Work From Home Handbook, 2008, Nolo, USA.

Cynthia C. Froggatt. Work Naked, 2001, Jossey-Bass, San Fransisco, USA.

Frances E. Kuo and William C. Sullivan. Aggression and Violence in the Inner City, 2001, Environment and Behavior, 33, 543-571.

Stephen B. Pociask, Joseph P. Fuhr Jr. Broadband Services: Economic and Environmental Benefits, 2007, The American Consumer Institute. Retrieved August 3, 2008, from: http://www.aci-citizenresearch.org/Final%20Green%20Benefits.pdf

Harold D. Stolovitch. Physical Environment Impacts Workplace Performance, 2007, Retrieved August 3, 2008, from: http://www.talentmgt.com/columnists/human-peformance/2007/December/487/index.php

Suzanne K. Vosburg. Mood and the Quantity and Quality of Ideas, 1998, Creativity Research Journal, 11, 315 – 324.

An Enriched Environment Stimulates An Increase In The Number Of Nerve Cells In Brains Of Older Mice. Salk Institute for Biological Studies, Press Release, April 24, 1997. Retrieved August 3, 2008, from: http://www.salk.edu/news/news_press_details.php?id=59

Goldman Sachs 2007 Environmental Report. Retrieved August 3, 2008, from:
http://www2.goldmansachs.com/citizenship/environment/Environmental-Report-2007.pdf

Computing Sustainability. In economist.com. Retrieved July 16, 2008, from:
http://www.economist.com/research/articlesbysubject/displaystory.cfm?subjectid=348909&story_id=11585208

Mood Linked To Cognitive Abilities, Washington University In St. Louis, Press Release 19 March 2002. Retrieved August 3, 2008, from: http://nootropics.com/mood/

4. *KEYS TO FREEDOM*

E. Glenn Schellenberg, Takayuki Nakata, Patrick G. Hunter, Sachiko Tamoto. Exposure to music and cognitive performance: tests of children and adults, 2007, Psychology of Music, 35, 5-19.

5. *WHY PAPERLESS IS BETTER*

IDC Expert: Preparing Your Organization for a Growing Mobile Workforce.
Retrieved August 3, 2008, from:
http://whitepapers.zdnet.com/abstract.aspx?docid=356957

6. *ADDRESSING CRITICS OF THE PAPERLESS OFFICE*

A.J. Sellen and R.H.R. Harper. The myth of the paperless office, 2003, MIT Press, Cambridge, MA, USA.

Enriching the Desktop Metaphor with Physics, Piles and the Pen. Thesis by Anand Agarawala. Graduate Department of Computer Science University of Toronto.
Retrieved August 3, 2008, from:
http://www.dgp.toronto.edu/~anand/big/Thesis-BumpTop.pdf

Erasable paper—nice idea, no market? In The Economist online. Retrieved July 16, 2008, from:
http://www.economist.com/daily/columns/techview/displaystory.cfm?story_id=11354488

7. *PROFESSIONAL AND PERSONAL GROWTH WITH ICT*

Researchers: Video games benefit seniors. Miamiherald.com. Retrieved August 3, 2008, from:
http://www.miamiherald.com/business/story/552868.html

Brain games aim to boost your IQ. BBC News. Retrieved August 3, 2008, from: http://news.bbc.co.uk/1/hi/technology/4930996.stm

8. *ICT AND RELATIONSHIPS: PROCEED WITH CAUTION*

Maressa H. Orzack. Computer Addiction: What Is It? 1998, Psychiatric Times, 15.
Retrieved August 3, 2008, from:
http://www.psychiatrictimes.com/display/article/10168/54286

Hooked on the Web: Help Is on the Way. New York Times December 1, 2005. Retrieved August 3, 2008, from:
http://www.nytimes.com/2005/12/01/fashion/thursdaystyles/01addict.html?pagewanted=print

Computer addiction. Wikipedia. Retrieved August 3, 2008, from:

http://en.wikipedia.org/wiki/Computer_addiction

9. *FIRST, COMMITMENT. THEN, FREEDOM*

Procrastination. Wikipedia. Retrieved August 3, 2008, from: http://en.wikipedia.org/wiki/Procrastination

Procrastination. Retrieved August 3, 2008, from: http://www.unc.edu/depts/wcweb/handouts/procrastination.html

How To Stop Procrastinating. Retrieved August 3, 2008, from: http://www.getmoredone.com/tips2.html

10. *PAPERLESS TELECOMMUTING & VIRTUAL, DISPERSED TEAMS*

Telecommuting. Wikipedia. Retrieved July 16, 2008, from: http://en.wikipedia.org/wiki/Telecommuting

Ten Advantages to Telecommuting. Gilgordon.com. Retrieved July 16, 2008, from: http://www.gilgordon.com/telecommutesafe/telebenefits.html

Professor Albert Mehrabian's communications model. businessballs.com. Retrieved July 16, 2008, from: http://www.businessballs.com/mehrabiancommunications.htm

Telework (Telecommuting): the Benefits - and some Issues! In eto.org.uk. Retrieved July 16, 2008, from: http://www.eto.org.uk/faq/faq03.htm

The Telecommuting Trend. Allearnatives.com. Retrieved July 16, 2008, from: http://www.allearnatives.com/telecommuting/trend3.asp

Kelli A. Green, Mayra López, Allen Wysocki, and Karl Kepner. Telecommuting as a True Workplace Alternative. University of Florida. Retrieved July 16, 2008, from: http://edis.ifas.ufl.edu/HR021

11. *PAPERLESS PROS AND CONS FOR CORPORATIONS*

Christa Heibel. Benefits of implementing a telecommuting program. Businessvoip.tmcnet.com. Retrieved July 16, 2008, from: http://businessvoip.tmcnet.com/topics/benefits/articles/16146-benefits-telecommuting.htm>

Virtual teams. Seanet.com. Retrieved July 16, 2008, from: http://www.seanet.com/~daveg/vrteams.htm

Trends leading to virtual teams. Seanet.com. Retrieved July 16, 2008, from http://www.seanet.com/~daveg/articles.htm>

Transforming the workforce. IBM Global Business Services, IBM Institute for Business Value 2007.

12. *GLOBAL DEVELOPMENT AND HEALTH THROUGH ICT*

Ken Banks and Richard Burge. Mobile Phones: An Appropriate Tool For Conservation And Development? 2004, Fauna & Flora International, Cambridge, UK. Copyright 2004 ISBN: 1-903703-15-8. Retrieved August 16, 2008, from: http://www.kiwanja.net/database/document/report_ffi_vodafone_icts.pdf

Rhett Butler. Cell phones may help "save" Africa, 2005, Mongabay.com. Retrieved August 16, 2008, from: http://news.mongabay.com/2005/0712-rhett_butler.html

Can the Cellphone Help End Global Poverty? NY Times Online. Retrieved July 16, 2008, from: http://www.nytimes.com/2008/04/13/magazine/13anthropology-t.html

Tech Progress Helps Developing Countries Reduce Poverty. Retrieved August 16, 2008, from: http://web.worldbank.org/WBSITE/EXTERNAL/NEWS/0,,contentMDK:21606738~pagePK:64257043~piPK:437376~theSitePK:4607,00.html

Mobile Phone Use In Developing Countries. Retrieved August 16, 2008, from:
http://www.strategicdigitaloutreach.com/index.php/v2/permalink/mobile_phone_use_in_developing_countries/

Mobile Internet for Developing Countries. By Michael Minges for the International Telecommunication Union. Retrieved August 16, 2008, from: http://www.isoc.org/inet2001/CD_proceedings/G53/mobilepaper2.htm

13. *PRACTICAL GUIDE FOR GOING PAPERLESS*

David M. Kaufmann. How To Setup A "Paperless" Office –You Can Do It And Save Money. Copyright 2002-2006. Denver Tax Software, Inc, Denver, Colorado. Retrieved August 16, 2008, from: http://denvertax.com

Made in the USA
Monee, IL
14 September 2026

63198307R00089